150 DRIBBLING GAMES FOR SOCCER

Nicola Pica

**Library of Congress
Cataloging - in - Publication Data**

150 Dribbling Games for Soccer
Nicola Pica

ISBN No. 1-59164-063-6
Lib. of Congress Catalog No. 2003094472
© 2003

Editing
Bryan R. Beaver

Reedswain Publishing
88 Wells Road
Spring City, PA 19475
800.331.5191
www.reedswain.com
info@reedswain.com

Every child who practices a sport dreams of winning and of experiencing moments of glory. But what counts is to play, to be together, and to get involved so that in a contest you give your best.

The activities proposed in this book are useful and entertaining means to enable players to reach these objectives. The author has put together a coaching project. "Dribbling the ball" is the coaching means used here to develop general coordination and to consolidate balance and the other skills.

I am deeply convinced that the players can carry out the following useful exercises without becoming bored. As the Italian writer Gianni Rodari said, "for a child, is it worth learning while crying what can be learned while enjoying oneself?".

Umberto Tarantino
Teacher at Rome
 "Tor Vergata" University

Following on his book "Un gioco e via", published in 1998 by Edizioni Nuova Prhomos (and published in English by Reedswain under the title "120 Competitive Games and Training Exercises"), Nicola Pica presents here a new collection of games and exercises focused on dribbling the ball, which is a useful source for practical drills. Aware of his coaching competence, demonstrated during the courses for soccer coaches organized by our Provincial Board, I would like to emphasize in particular the originality of the exercises proposed.

Gerardo Trombetta
President of Federazione Calcio Caserta

FOREWORD

This is not a theoretical book, it is a handbook which contains exercises focused on "dribbling the ball", in which the players are required to:

- listen
- compete
- report

with the objective of improving motor dexterity.

Dexterity implies several motor skills:

- knowledge of one's own body in its totality: the ability to perceive one's own body position in space;
- balance: the ability to keep in balance the body's various bone segments when they go through postural adaptations;
- space-time coordination: motor organization, in its global execution, taking space and time into consideration. The development of this kind of coordination in team sports is important, since the movements with and without the ball, as well as the paths of passes and shots and the sense of position, develop in time, according to a certain pace, and in a given space;
- lateralization: man is the only living being whose perceptive and motor skills follow the principle of laterality; in fact, in using his limbs he can be either right-handed or left-handed. Therefore, it is important to carry out the various exercises and to improve the movements with both the right and left hand and foot.

While the players learn the technical skill of dribbling the ball, they also acquire the use of abilities which imply the development of coordination processes; such abilities are also objectives to be accomplished with young players. In fact,

- we can define "ability" as "the capacity to be able". In the case of the soccer player, this means the capacity to acquire those ways of moving which are specific to soccer.
- These abilities cooperate with one another and coexist in a player, thereby "toughening" him.
- The technical and tactical aspects of soccer are interdependent with the ability.
- The abilities are needed by the children between 7 and 14.

"Coordination" ability enables a child to reach a richer and more harmonious ability to move, helping him to establish space relations among external objects as well as between the external objects and his own body. In addition, for a child, a good "space-time" organization is a fundamental and functional determinant to learning basic technical content.

The age of puberty is really a difficult period for a child, who faces a physical, motor and psychological transformation. He is often disharmonious and must gain back his motor control, which was lost due to the rapid growth of his limbs.

His temperament fluctuates between two extreme poles, joy and sadness. As

Giovanni De Toni puts it, "the pubescent boy or girl is fundamentally an incautious intro-
vert, unable of extroversion".

- In everyday life there are many occasions where we use coordination processes. For
  example, the use of a computer requires a coordination process which involves thought
  and eye-hand coordination (the fingers that give shape to thoughts on the keyboard), in
  order to control the outcome.
- The widespread use of computers and television is influencing our culture and our ideas,

and is changing children's habits. Most of them share the concept of "communicating
without having to get together". It is especially for them that relational and competitive
games acquire extreme importance, since they contain an associating drive and teach
respect for common rules. According to Francesco Fabbroni, play is a natural intermedi-
ary which helps children learn spontaneously.

The increase in behavior and motor abilities increases the children's ability to do more.
This book contains exercises that belong to two different levels of difficulty, which, in a
proper coaching progression, correspond to part one and part two.

TALKING ABOUT ONESELF - ONE
(first coaching session at the beginning of the season)

OBJECTIVES	Listening. Watching.
EQUIPMENT	One ball per player.
AREA OF PLAY	Any area of the field.
PLAYERS	They sit on the ground, forming a half-circle.
COACH	He sits on the ground with the players.
ACTIVITY	Keeping eye contact with the players, the coach briefly introduces himself. Then, he sets some rules of behavior:

- the players must listen to everybody's speech, watching the speaker as he speaks;
- before speaking, the players must wait for the teammate who is speaking to finish.

The coach asks one player at a time, in turns, to dribble the ball around his sitting teammates while watching their behavior as they talk about themselves. When the coach gives the signal, the player who is dribbling the ball stops the ball with his foot and says which of his teammates did not watch or did not listen to the player who was talking, and the coach gives them a red card. The game finishes when all the players have dribbled the ball. The winner is the player with fewest red cards.

WAY TO STOP THE BALL Under the sole of the foot.

TALKING ABOUT ONESELF - TWO
(first coaching session at the beginning of the season)

OBJECTIVES

Listening.
Watching.
Suggesting activities to introduce a technical content.

EQUIPMENT

Some balls.

AREA OF PLAY

Any area of the field.

PLAYERS

They sit on the ground, forming a half-circle.

COACH

He sits on the ground with the players.

ACTIVITY

In turns, each player explains how to carry out a game or a motor activity with which he is familiar (for example, because he knows it from school). In the meanwhile, the coach chooses one child whose task is to check that everybody watches and listens to the child that is speaking. This conversational activity permits the coach to get to know his players better. In order to get them more involved, he should let them play those games they have explained and which also have a technical content.

CONSIDERATIONS

To help the younger players, the coach should use the games with which they are familiar as a means of coaching technical content.

EXAMPLE

POISONED BALL

This is one of the most popular ball games among children, and is therefore one which is regularly suggested. The players are divided into two teams. One team is arranged in the goal area and the other is arranged outside the goal area. Each player outside the goal area has a ball. When the coach gives the signal, the players outside the goal area throw the ball with their hands, trying to hit one of the players inside the goal area. Of course, the latter move or bend to avoid being hit. Each time a player is hit, the throwing team scores a point. After a pre-established period of time, the teams change roles.

According to the players' level of ability, the coach may ask them to drop the ball from their hands and kick it with the instep to hit the players inside the goal area, or, at a more advanced level, he may ask them to drop-kick the ball.

GETTING TO KNOW ONE ANOTHER

OBJECTIVES

Space structuring.
Learning one another's names.

EQUIPMENT

One ball per player.
A balloon for the coach.

AREA OF PLAY

Penalty area.
Small goals are formed along the long side of the goal area by using cones.

PLAYERS

They are in the goal area.

COACH

He is 5-6 yards away from the small goals.

ACTIVITY

The players dribble the ball in the goal area, arms out stretched, trying not to touch one another. The coach throws his ball upward and calls out one name. The player, or players, with that name dribble the ball inside one small goal and stop it there, then run to catch the balloon thrown by the coach. The others stop themselves.

WAY TO DRIBBLE

The ball must be touched at every step.

WAY TO STOP THE BALL Under the sole of the foot.

GATHERING - ONE

OBJECTIVES   Awareness of the playing space.

EQUIPMENT   One ball per player.
A few cones.

AREA OF PLAY   Goal area.
Two cones are used to mark two corners, A and B, while two other cones are used to mark an imaginary line, C, connecting them.

ACTIVITY

1. The players gather around corner A. When the coach gives the signal, they start to dribble the ball inside the goal area, arms outstretched, trying not to touch one another.
   When the coach gives another signal, they go back to corner A and gather around it.
2. The players gather around corner B. When the coach gives the signal, they all, one after the other, dribble the ball along the perimeter of the goal area. When the coach gives another signal, they all go back to corner B.
3. The players gather around corner B. When the coach gives the signal, they arrange themselves at each other's side along line C, while dribbling the ball.
4. The players are divided into two groups, and each group gathers around one corner. When the coach gives the signal, both groups arrange themselves along line C, one behind the other.

WAY TO DRIBBLE   The ball must be touched at every step.

GATHERING - TWO

OBJECTIVES

Awareness of the playing space.
Space-time structuring.

EQUIPMENT

One ball per player.
A few cones.
Various items of equipment.

AREA OF PLAY

A smaller size field; the cones are used to mark some spaces in each of which there is a different piece of equipment.

ACTIVITY

1. The players gather around one marked space. When the coach gives the signal, they start to dribble the ball first along the longer side of the field, and then along the shorter one, back and forth.
Then, the coach calls out the name of an item of equipment and they dribble the ball to the space where it has been placed.
2. The players gather around one marked space. When the coach gives the first signal, they all start dribbling the ball wherever they want. When the coach gives the second signal, they all stop. When the coach gives the next signal (the name of an item of equipment) they all dribble the ball to the space where that item has been placed.
3. The players dribble the ball wherever they want, but within the goal area of the smaller size field. When the coach gives the signal, they stop and stretch out their arms, trying not to touch each other.
4. The players are all gathered inside one of the spaces marked by the cones, holding hands. When the coach gives the signal, they stop holding hands and start dribbling the ball back, inside the penalty area of the smaller size field, trying not to touch each other. When the coach gives the next signal, they go back to the original place and hold hands again.

WAY TO DRIBBLE

A. Forward: the ball must be touched at every step with the right and with the left foot, alternately.
B. Back: the ball must be stopped under the sole of the foot or with the inside of the foot, according to the coach's instructions, and then must be dribbled back while hopping on the supporting leg.

IN LINE - ONE

OBJECTIVE Space-time structuring.

EQUIPMENT One ball per player.

ACTIVITY

1. The players line up, at a distance of 2-3 yards from each other. The first person in line dribbles the ball in any direction. The others follow him while dribbling the ball too, trying to remain in line. When the coach gives the signal, the first player in line stops the ball and does any exercise he wants. For example, he may jump, turn a somersault, squat, roll on the ground, etc. The other players imitate him. Those who make a mistake do not participate in the next exercise. When the coach gives the next signal, the players line up with the ball again and the game re-starts. After two or three repetitions, a different player is selected to be the first player in line.

2. Practicing with one foot at a time, the players dribble the ball around the field in the direction shown by the coach. When the coach shows a number with his fingers, say 3 or 4, the players must form 3- or 4-player lines along the lines of the field.

3. The players line up around the goal area. The last player in line has a plastic tape hanging out from the back of his shorts, as if it were a tail. When the coach gives the signal, the players start to dribble the ball along the lines of the perimeter of the goal area, remaining in line. The first player in line must try to dribble fast in order to touch the tail of the last player in line. If he touches, then the last player in line goes to the front of the line in the next repetition.

4. Several lines of 4 or 5 players each are formed. In each line, the first player has a ball and dribbles it around the field, touching it at every step, while the other players in his line follow him. When the coach gives the signal, the first player in each line kicks the ball softly forward or sideways, and immediately goes to the back of the line; the second player in each line runs to the ball kicked by the teammate who now has gone to the back of the line, and dribbles it forward. Some hurdles can be placed randomly on the field. If two lines meet, the first player of each line is substituted.

"LOOK AT THE FREE SPACE"

OBJECTIVE

Space global structuring.

EQUIPMENT

One ball per player.
A few cones.

AREA OF PLAY

The midfield circle.
The cones are used to mark as many irregular and unequal spaces as the number of groups involved. These spaces are about 10 yards from the midfield line.

PLAYERS

The players are divided into two or more groups, according to the number of participants.

ACTIVITY

The coach assigns each group a space that the group must occupy at the end of the exercise. All of the players are arranged along the midfield line, with the assigned space at their back. When the coach gives the signal, they dribble the ball toward the direction that the coach shows with his arms. When he gives another signal, the players stop and put the sole of their foot on the ball, turn around and dribble the ball toward the assigned space. Each player places himself inside the assigned space so as to allow his group optimum arrangement. The group that is arranged better in the assigned space, that is, the group that leaves less empty space, scores a point.
The exercise is repeated several times, and each time each group is assigned a different space.

WAY TO DRIBBLE

A. When dribbling the ball toward the direction shown by the coach, practice with one foot at a time.
B. When dribbling the ball toward the assigned spaces and when dribbling it back to the midfield line, the ball must be touched at every step.

"CALL YOUR TEAMMATES"

OBJECTIVES

Space structuring.
Visual coordination.
Learning one another's names.

EQUIPMENT

One ball per player.
A few cones.
Small items of equipment and various objects.

AREA OF PLAY

The penalty area.
The cones are used to mark two rectangular spaces (A and A1) on the field, at a certain distance from each other. In zone K, which is the zone between the two rectangular spaces, various objects and small items of equipment are placed to form small goals. Each goal is different from the others because it is composed of different things (i.e., one bag and a cone, two bags, two hurdles, one hurdle and a pole, etc.).
Also in space A1, small goals identical to the ones in zone K are formed.

ACTIVITY

Each player dribbles the ball forward within space A, arms outstretched, without getting in his teammates' way. In turns, one player, called player "C", places himself inside space A1 and calls his teammates, one at a time, while moving to a different small goal in A1 each time he calls a teammate. The player who is called leaves space A and dribbles the ball forward across zone K, to space A1. When he crosses zone K, he must dribble the ball through the small goal which is identical to the one near which his teammate C was when he called him. Once in space A1, he keeps on dribbling the ball.

WAY TO DRIBBLE

The ball must be touched at every step.

"GET CLOSE TO YOUR TEAMMATE" - ONE

OBJECTIVE

Becoming aware of the space occupied by one's own body .

EQUIPMENT

One ball per player.
Mats scattered over the field.

AREA OF PLAY

The penalty area.

ACTIVITY

1. The players are arranged in a row on one side of the field. When the coach gives the signal, they dribble the ball as far as the mats and stop the ball; then, in pairs (each player forms a pair with the teammate who is closest to him at that moment), they lie down on a mat.
2. The players dribble the ball about the field in the directions shown by the coach.
   When the coach gives the signal, the players, in groups of three or four, stand first on a mat, then under it by holding it up on the palms of their hands.
3. The mats are arranged in twos or threes next to one another along the long side of the field. The players dribble the ball about the field, using one foot at a time. When the coach gives the signal, they stop the ball near the mats and lie down on the sets of mats in free groups, trying to fit as many as possible on each set.

"CHANGE YOUR PLACE"

OBJECTIVES
Space structuring.
Watching.
Body scheme.

EQUIPMENT
One ball per player.
Hurdles.

AREA OF PLAY
The goal area.
A small zone is marked at each of the four corners, by arranging the hurdles in a circle.

PLAYERS
The players are divided into four groups.

ACTIVITY
Each group is placed in one of the four small zones. All the players dribble the ball in the direction shown by the coach, with their arms outstretched, using one foot at a time. When the coach gives the signal, the players crawl under the hurdles after first passing the ball under the hurdle. Then, they dribble it again to another small zone, assigned to them by the coach. The group which is the first to enter the assigned zone scores a point.

"GET CLOSE TO YOUR TEAMMATE" - TWO

OBJECTIVE

Becoming aware of the space occupied by one's own body.

EQUIPMENT

One ball per player.
Some small balls.

AREA OF PLAY

The penalty area.

ACTIVITY

1. The players are arranged in a circle and hold hands. When the coach gives the signal, they dribble the ball forward, tightening the circle and getting closer, till they occupy the smallest space possible. When the coach gives the second signal, the players move backwards to their starting position, still hand in hand, dribbling the ball back with the sole of the foot (for example, the left foot) and hopping on the other leg.
2. In pairs, the players place themselves along each of the short sides of the penalty area, each player opposite the player with whom he has been paired (his "partner"). When the coach gives the signal, each player starts dribbling the ball toward his partner until he touches him; then he turns around and dribbles the ball back to the starting point.
3. The players place themselves in the middle of the penalty area, as close as possible to one another. By using some small balls, the coach marks the space (A) occupied by the players and marks a small 1-yard wide corridor (A1) to exit that space. When the coach gives the signal, the players move out of their space, one by one, along the narrow corridor (A1) and dribble the ball along the sides of the goal area. After all of them have exited space A, the coach gives a second signal; then the players dribble the ball into corridor A1 and go back into space A.

WAY TO DRIBBLE

The ball must be touched at every step.

"PULL THE TAIL AWAY" - ONE

OBJECTIVES

Familiarizing oneself with the ball.
Getting used to the observance of rules.

EQUIPMENT

One ball and a piece of plastic tape per player.
Some small balls.

AREA OF PLAY

The penalty area.

ACTIVITY

Each player has a plastic tape hanging out from the back of his shorts, as if it were a tail. While dribbling the ball around the field, the players try to pull the others' tails away, taking care not to lose their own. The exercise ends when all the players are left without tails. The winner is the player who has managed to pull away the most tails.

VARIATION

OBJECTIVE

Stimulating visualization.
Getting used to the observance of the rules.

PLAYERS

The players are divided into three teams: A, B and C.

ACTIVITY

The coach gives the signal and starts counting aloud from 1 to 60. Each player tries to pull the others' tail away, trying not to lose his own. When he finishes counting, the coach stops the game; the two teams with the highest number of players who have managed to keep their tail are the winners and score one point.

THE SQUARE GAME

OBJECTIVES

Space structuring.
Watching.

EQUIPMENT

One ball per player.
Cones, small items of equipment and various objects.

AREA OF PLAY

The penalty area.
About ten yards away from the long side of the goal area, square spaces are formed with cones, equal in number to the number of groups of players.

PLAYERS

The players are divided into several groups.

ACTIVITY

The coach assigns each group a small piece of equipment, which stands for the group, and a square space for that group to occupy.
Using one foot at a time, all the players dribble the ball around the field in the directions shown by the coach. At irregular intervals, the coach takes hold of two pieces of equipment and the two groups to whom those pieces of equipment have been assigned must quickly dribble the ball into the small square they have been assigned, trying to occupy as much space as possible.
The group that is first to enter the square scores two points, while the group that manages to occupy its square space in the best way, leaving less empty space, scores one point.

ON ALL FOURS

OBJECTIVES

Perception of one's own body.
Control of the ball.
Spine mobility.

EQUIPMENT

Several balls, poles and cones.

AREA OF PLAY

The goal area.
Along one of the short sides of the goal area, square spaces are formed with cones, equal in number to the number of teams of players. An equal number of lines of poles are formed in the goal area; the poles are arranged in a cone-shaped way, as shown in the diagram below.

PLAYERS

The players are divided into three teams: A, B and C. Each team lines up opposite a square, with a line of poles at its back. Further behind the poles, there is an even number of balls for each team.

ACTIVITY

When the coach gives the signal, the last player in line from each team turns around and, passing through the cone-shaped poles, goes to take a ball. Once he has taken it, he has to take it to the square assigned to his team by going on all fours and pushing the ball forward with his knee. When he reaches the square, he leaves the ball there and goes, still on all fours, to the front of his line. At that moment, his teammate who is the last in line repeats the same exercise, and so on. The winner is the team that is the first to take all the balls into the square.

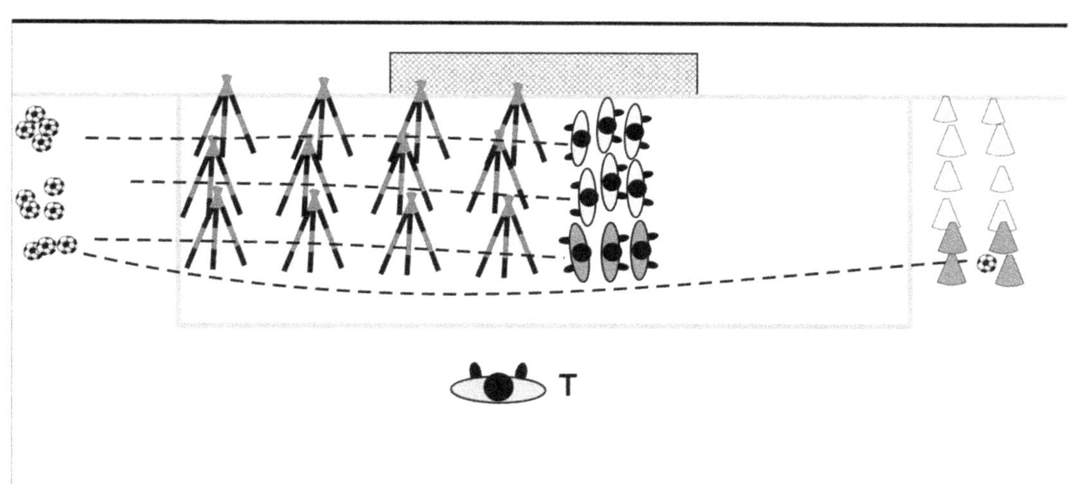
T

CONE-CARRIER - ONE

ACTIVITY

The teams start from the place where the balls were placed in the previous exercise, but this time cones replace the balls. Each player has a ball. When the coach gives the signal, the first player in line from each team puts a cone on the back of his "cone-carrier" teammate (the last in line from each team), who, on all fours, pushes the ball with his knee through the cone-shaped poles toward the assigned square. If the cone falls from his back, he stops and can re-start only after the first player in line has put it back onto his back.

When he reaches the assigned square, the "cone-carrier" drops it and, still on all fours, pushes the ball with his knee and goes to the front of his team's line. Once he reaches the front, the last player in line starts, and so on. The team that is the first to carry all its cones to the assigned square is the winner.

CONE-CARRIER - TWO

ACTIVITY

Each player is assigned a number.

The coach gets the game started by calling out two numbers; the first number refers to the number of cones the player must carry on his back into the designated square, and the second number specifies the player who will be the "cone-carrier". If, along the course, the "cone-carrier" drops the cones that he has on his back, he must stop and wait for a teammate to put them back onto his back. The player who is the first to carry the specified number of cones into the square scores a point.

TILE GAME

OBJECTIVES

Balance.
Control of the ball.

EQUIPMENT

Three 12-inch wooden floor tiles per team.
Poles and cones.

AREA OF PLAY

The goal area.
Along one of the short sides of the goal area, a zone (zone E) is marked with the poles. In this zone, other poles and cones are then arranged.

PLAYERS

The players are divided into three teams: A, B and C.

ACTIVITY

Each team is arranged in a line outside the sideline which is opposite to zone E. One player for each team, "A1", "B1" and "C1", places himself inside zone E. When the coach gives the signal, the task of these three players is to carry out individual exercises focused on controlling and familiarizing themselves with the ball. Meanwhile, the first person in each team's line must reach zone E by using his wooden tiles as follows: he puts them on the ground, about 12 inches from one another, and can walk only on them. Therefore, when he has his feet on the second and third tile, he must recover the first tile from behind and put it ahead of himself in order to move forward, and so on. Once he reaches zone E, he starts practicing the control of the ball; his teammate who was in that zone before, leaves it by using the tiles in the same way, going in the opposite direction back to the starting point. When he reaches the starting point, another teammate repeats the path to zone E on the tiles again, and so on until the last player of the team has carried out the exercise. The team whose players are the first to finish the course wins the repetition.

EXERCISES TO CONTROL THE BALL

1. A course with geometric figures (circles, squares, rectangles, etc.) is formed by laying poles and cones on their side on the ground. The players dribble the ball inside the geometric figure or along its perimeter, as follows: clockwise, with the outside of the right foot; then counter clockwise, with the outside of the left foot; then clockwise, with the inside of the left foot;

and, finally, counter clockwise, with the inside of the right foot.
2. The players dribble two balls at the same time.

3. The players dribble the ball around one or two cones.
4. The players dribble the ball zigzagging.
5. The players dribble the ball along a straight line.
6. The players dribble the ball along a straight line, stop it with the inside of the foot and start again, and so on until the end of the track.

IMPORTANT The players must not keep their eyes on the ball, they must only cast it a sidelong glance.

FINDING YOUR BEARINGS - ONE

OBJECTIVES

Finding one's bearings while moving
- forward-back;
- up-down;
- right-left.

Touching the ball purposefully.
Eye-hand coordination.

EQUIPMENT

One ball and one balloon per player.

AREA OF PLAY

The goal area.

PLAYERS

The players are placed in the goal area without a specific arrangement.

ACTIVITY

1. The players dribble the ball while pushing the balloon forward by hitting it upward with their hand.
2. The players dribble the ball forward, to the right and to the left, while pushing the balloon forward, keeping it low by hitting it softly with their hand. The ball should not get any higher than the waist. As an alternative, the balloon can be kept on the palm of the hand.
3. The players dribble the ball while keeping the balloon on the palm of their right hand. Then, they throw the balloon upward, pass under it while dribbling the ball with the inside or the outside of the foot, and catch the balloon on the palm of their left hand, and so on.
4. While they dribble the ball, the players throw the balloon forward and upward, pass under it and dribble the ball 3-4 yards forward, then turn around and with the same foot dribble the ball back and catch the balloon as close as possible to the ground, without letting it touch the ground.

The coach should require the players to keep an eye on the balloon while dribbling, so as to turn around at the precise moment to seize the balloon just before it touches the ground.

FINDING YOUR BEARINGS - TWO

OBJECTIVES

Finding one's bearings while moving
Improving the relationship with teammates.
Improving skills.

EQUIPMENT

One ball per player.

AREA OF PLAY

The penalty area.

PLAYERS

The players are divided into groups of three.

ACTIVITY

1. The groups of players place themselves along the lines about 4-5 yards from one another. Then, all players start to dribble the ball forward along the lines with the outside of the foot. When the coach gives the signal, the players stop and sit down in a row along one line, shoulder to shoulder. Then, all together, they raise their buttocks from the ground by placing their hands under themselves and propping themselves up from the ground. They move forward and back in this "reverse crab" position, calling out "let's go forward" and "let's go back" to coordinate their movement.

2. The various groups of players place themselves along the lines of the penalty area 4-5 yards from one another. Practicing with only one foot at a time, they dribble the ball to the left or to the right of the line. When they dribble the ball to the right, they touch it with the inside of the tip of the left foot (or with the outside of the tip of the right foot). When they dribble the ball to the left, they touch it with the outside of the tip of the left foot (or with the inside of the tip of the right foot). When the coach gives the signal, the players stop and two players from each group kneel down opposite each other and roll a third teammate who is lying on his back between them, while they call out "forward" and "back" to coordinate their movement. When the coach gives the next signal, the roles are exchanged.

3. In line, the groups dribble the ball with one foot along the lines of the penalty area, to the right and then to the left. When the coach gives a visual signal, all the players stop the ball with the inside of the foot. Then they turn around and re-dribble the ball with the inside or with the outside of the other foot.

When the coach gives a voice signal, the groups stop again; two players from each group place themselves opposite each other while the third player from each group stands between them, rigid as a pole. The two players make the player sway by pushing him back and forth, with their hands wide open and their legs slightly bent in order to better support him at his shoulders, all the while increasing the distance between them. When the coach gives the next signal, the roles are exchanged.

FINDING YOUR BEARINGS - THREE

OBJECTIVES

Finding one's bearings while moving forward-back.
Improving the relationship with the teammates.
Control of the ball.

EQUIPMENT

One ball per player.
Cones.
Bags, chairs and hurdles.

AREA OF PLAY

The penalty area.
In the goal area, cones are used to form as many small squares as there are pairs of players. Chairs, bags and hurdles are put randomly on the field to make dribbling the ball more difficult.

PLAYERS

The players are divided into pairs.

ACTIVITY

1. The coach moves around the field. The players dribble the ball and copy his movements, standing either behind or opposite him, according to his orders.
2. The coach moves about the penalty area. The players are in pairs, opposite him, and follow his movements while they dribble the ball. When the coach gives a voice signal, each pair moves into a small square. One of the pair stops the ball and pretends to hit his teammate on the back, on the thighs, on the buttocks and on the shoulders. The latter continues to control the ball while avoiding the "hits" with quick movements.
3. The coach moves about the field. The players dribble the ball behind him. When the coach gives the signal, the players go to the goal area and place themselves opposite one another in pairs. One of each pair guides the other, with his voice and gestures, to help him dribble the ball back. The ball is dribbled back by rolling it back with one foot, while hopping on the supporting leg.

IN LINE - TWO

OBJECTIVES

Body scheme.
Changing direction with the outside of the foot.
Touching the ball.

EQUIPMENT

One ball per player.

AREA OF PLAY

The penalty area.

PLAYERS

The players are divided into groups of three or four players each.

ACTIVITY

1. The groups are arranged at a distance of 4-5 yards from one another, along the lines of the field. Each player in a line faces the back of his teammate. They dribble the ball forward along the line. When the coach gives the signal, all the players stop, place their legs wide apart and stretch out their arms, placing them on the shoulders of the teammate in front of them. The last player in each line goes on all fours and pushes the ball forward, passing under his teammates' legs, and when he reaches the front of his line he stands up and places his legs wide open. The exercise continues until all the players have passed under "tunnel".

2. The groups are arranged at a distance of 4-5 yards from one another, each player in the line facing the back of the teammate in front of him, and each dribbles the ball forward to the right and to the left of the line on which they were arranged, alternatively using the outside and then the inside of the right foot. When the coach gives the signal, the players turn around to the right while dribbling the ball with the outside of the right foot, and continue to dribble the ball in the new direction with the outside and then with the inside of the left foot. The turn to the right is carried out as follows: soon after touching the ball with the right foot, the players place the inside of their left foot next to the ball, as if intending to kick it with the right foot. They stop the movement of the ball with the outside of the right foot, and turn around by pivoting on the right leg; then they dribble the ball in the new direction with their left foot. The opposite sequence is used to carry out the turn to the left.

3. The players are divided into pairs. The players in each
   pair are "connected" by a stick, with each player holding an end. The pairs are placed in line at a distance of
   4-5 yards separating each pair, and, holding the stick as
   explained above, each pair dribbles the ball forward to
   the right and then to the left of the line on which they
   started, alternatively using the outside and then the
   inside of the right foot. When the coach gives the
   signal, the pairs stop the ball with the sole of their
   right foot, and start dribbling it forward with the inside
   and then with the outside of their left foot.

IN LINE - THREE

OBJECTIVES

Improving relationships with teammates.
Developing balance skills.

EQUIPMENT

One ball per player.
Cones, poles, benches, mats.
Various objects : bags, chairs, etc.

AREA OF PLAY

The penalty area.
The following objects are placed inside the penalty area for each group: a bench, a line of cones, two poles and a mat. Also, a few narrow "corridors" are marked with various objects and items of equipment.

PLAYERS

The players are divided into groups of three players each.

ACTIVITY

All the groups are lined up together; each player dribbles the ball forward, following the movements of the coach, who is the first in line and makes sudden winding and sharp turns, changes the pace of the run (slow-fast), stops, re-starts.
When the players are close to the mats, the coach yells "stop". One player per group lies down on the mat; his two teammates wrap him up in the mat and roll him forward. When the coach yells "go", each player goes back to his position in the line. When the coach calls out the next "stop", the roles in each group are exchanged, and so on.
After carrying out this exercise a certain number of times, the coach calls out "contact": the players place themselves in a circle, each with his own body in contact with the body of the teammate next to him. While keeping this "contact", all the players sit down and then stand up. When the coach calls out "go", the players recover their position in the line and start dribbling the ball forward again. The coach may give the "contact" signal several times, and each time the players must carry out one of the following exercises while in a circle and in physical "contact" with each other.
When the coach calls out "stop" near the benches, each group carries out a balance exercise, which must be different each time.

<table>
<tr><td>"CONTACT" EXERCISES</td><td>

- In a circle, hops on the spot.
- One player in each group lies down on his back while his two teammates seize him by his arms and drag him.
- All the players lie down on their backs and form a three-player line on the ground (in each group, two players are in contact with each other's hands, while feet of the third player are in contact with the feet of one of the other two teammates): from this position, they roll to their side.
- All the players lie down on their stomachs, next to each other, except the players of one group, who roll on them. The group that rolls is continuously changed.
- The players of each group lie down on their backs forming a three-player line on the ground; in each group, two players are in contact with each other's head, while the feet of the third player are in contact with the feet of one of the other two teammates. From this position, they roll to their side.
- Two players in each group lift their teammate by holding him by the feet and by the shoulders, and swing him.
- All the players form a line while keeping their legs wide apart in order to make a "tunnel"; the last player in the line, on all fours, passes through the "tunnel" pushing the ball forward.

</td></tr>
</table>

the

<table>
<tr><td>BALANCE EXERCISES</td><td>

- Each group is given a bench; a line of cones is formed on the bench, laying the cones on their side; the players of the group must walk on the line of cones.
- Each group places two sticks on the bench assigned to the group; taking turns, the players of the group climb on the bench and walk on the sticks, making them roll back and forth.
- The players throw the ball up and then catch it while standing on the bench on only one leg.
- In each group, one player walks on the bench while his two teammates pass the ball to each other (using a header, they can pass each other one ball, or, using their hands, they can pass each other two balls at the same time) all the while moving along the side of the bench, avoiding hitting their teammate walking on the bench.
- While standing on the bench, the players must take off one shoe.
- While one player is standing on the bench, his two teammates lift the bench and move it up and down or forward and back.

</td></tr>
</table>

- While one player is standing on the bench, he receives the ball from either of his two teammates who are on the ground beside the bench; then he returns them the ball.
- While walking on the bench, the player must avoid the ball headed at him by either of his two teammates, who are on the ground on either side of the bench.
- While walking on the bench, the player bounces the ball (like in basketball).
- In each group, two players are on all fours next to each other, and move slowly. The third player stands on their backs, legs wide apart, trying to keep his balance.

NOTE The line should not be considered a formal order; it is rather an organization of space.

NAMES

OBJECTIVES

Learning to take turns.
Familiarizing with the group.
Touching the ball purposefully.

EQUIPMENT

One ball per player.

AREA OF PLAY

The penalty area.

PLAYERS

The players are arranged in a circle.

ACTIVITY

1. One player, player "A", places himself in the center of the circle. Taking turns, the other players dribble the ball around the circle, clockwise (first with the outside of the right foot and then with the inside of the left foot) or counter clockwise (first with the outside of the left foot and then with the inside of the right foot), according to the direction called out by the coach. Meanwhile, player "A" is making various movements - lying on his stomach, then on his back, then going on all fours, on his knees, etc. While the others dribble the ball around the circle, they call out their own name and each position that player "A" takes. Player "A" is replaced after all the players have dribbled the ball around the circle.

2. A square marked by four cones, is made inside a circle. When the coach gives the signal, one player, "A", dribbles the ball forward into the square by touching it at every step. "A" stops in front of one cone with the ball between his feet and calls out his name. Then, he slightly touches the ball with the inside of his right foot, so that the ball passes behind his left leg. "A" turns around by pivoting on his left foot and dribbles the ball to the cone on his left. He stops when he is at the cone, calls out his name again and so on until he has done this with each of the four cones. Then, he goes back to his initial position and the teammate on his left repeats the exercise. After everybody has carried out the exercise, the exercise is carried out again, this time to the right.

3. Player "A" has a ball at his feet and holds another ball in his hands. While he dribbles the ball, every now and then he calls out his name and at the same time throws ball in his hands upward and forward and catches it before it touches the ground. When the coach calls out

the name of a teammate, "A" passes the ball in his hands to the teammate whose name has been called and goes back to his place, while his teammate repeats the exercise that "A" has just done.

The coach must require the players to dribble the ball forward with only one touch as they move forward to catch the ball they have thrown in the air; as they catch the ball in the air, they can stop the ball they have at their feet with the sole of the foot or with the inside of the foot that has kicked it, and then restart dribbling it with the other foot after they have caught the other ball.

4. When the coach gives the signal, two players at a time ("A" and "B", opposite each other) call each other and, while dribbling the ball at the same time, exchange places.

All players carry out this exercise in turns.

VARIATION TO POINT 4

Groups of four/five players exchange places:
- each player calls out the name of the player opposite him;
- in turns, one player in one of the two groups, or one player in each group, calls out the names of the players with whom his group is exchanging places.

WITHSTANDING THE PACE

OBJECTIVES

Knowing one's limits.
Learning to withstand the pace.

EQUIPMENT

One ball per player.

AREA OF PLAY

The penalty area.

PLAYERS

The players can be arranged in groups, or individually, or in pairs.

1. The players are divided into three or four-player groups. One group at a time dribbles the ball, touching it at every step, while the coach "beats time" by counting up to 20. The ball must be touched based on the sequence of the numbers: with the left foot when the number is uneven, with the right foot when the number is even.
2. Individual exercise: one player at a time dribbles the ball while counting up to 20 and touching the ball at every step, with the left foot when the number is uneven and with the right foot when the number is even.
3. The players are divided into three or four-player groups. One group at a time dribbles the ball while counting. The player who can count for the longest time without stopping continues the exercise with the following group.
4. The players are divided into pairs. When the coach gives the signal, one pair at a time dribbles the ball forward as far as an obstacle which is placed a certain distance away from the starting point. From there, the pair must go back to the starting point, still dribbling the ball, trying to get to it before the coach has counted up to 20 (or 30, depending on the players' skills). If successful, the pair continues the exercise with the next pair.

IN CONTACT

OBJECTIVES

Building relationships.

EQUIPMENT

One ball per player.

AREA OF PLAY

The penalty area.

PLAYERS

The players are arranged in a circle, in a row, or in pairs.

ACTIVITY

1. In a circle. Each player, in turn, dribbles the ball along the outside of the circle formed by his teammates, passing so close to them as to almost touch them. While he dribbles the ball, the player calls out his name and then the name of a teammate, ordering him: "I would like you not to…", and then "I would like you to…", asking him whatever he wants him to do, while the teammate listens and does what he is asked.
2. In a row, along one of the short sides of the field. When the coach gives the signal, the players dribble the ball toward the opposite side. When the coach gives a pre-established signal, each player, with his arms, contacts the teammates that are next to him or in front of him, and continues to dribble the ball. When the coach gives the next signal, the players stop touching each other and continue to dribble the ball, and so on.
3. In pairs, next to each other, along one of the short sides of the field, holding hands. One player in the pair, for example, player "A", puts his right foot between the legs of his teammate "B", while "B" puts his left foot between "A"'s legs. When the coach gives the signal, "A" dribbles the ball forward with his left foot and "B" with his right foot.

ADVICE

We recommend that, when possible, the pairs be formed with players that have not yet established relationships with each other, so that new friends can be made.

OPPOSING YOUR OWN TEAMMATE

OBJECTIVES
Training strength.
Dribbling the ball around a circle.

EQUIPMENT
One ball for every "number 3" player.

AREA OF PLAY
The penalty area.

PLAYERS
The players, numbered from 1 to 3, are divided into groups.

One group is formed by all the "number 1" players, arranged in a circle inside another circle formed by all the "number 2" players, which is in turn inside another circle formed by all the "number 3" players.

The "number 1" and "number 2" players carry out exercises in pairs; if there are extra players, they move to the circle of "number 3" players.

Every now and then, "number 3" players exchange places with "number 1" and "number 2" players.

ACTIVITY
"Number 3" players dribble the ball clockwise or counter clockwise (based on the coach's directions) around the concentric circles formed by "number 2" and "number 1" players. "Number 1" and "number 2" players, in pairs, carry out opposition exercises, as follows:

OPPOSITION EXERCISES

- Opposite each other, sitting on the ground with legs crossed, arms outstretched and palms of the hands against each other, each player tries to push the other to the ground.
- Lying on their stomachs, opposite each other, they arm wrestle. Or, one of them keeps his fists closed while the other tries to open them.
- Sitting on the ground, legs crossed, back to back, they push against each other.
- The same exercise as above, carried out in a standing position.
- Standing, with the palms of the hands against each other, they push each other.
- Lying on their stomachs, opposite each other, one of them holds one ball tightly in his hands while the other tries to take it away from him.
- Lying on their backs, soles of the foot against each other, one player holds one ball between his ankles while the other tries to pull it away from him with his feet.

- On their knees, opposite each other, they catch each other with their outstretched arms and try to push each other back.
- Opposite each other, one is sitting with legs crossed and the other is standing; the latter pulls his teammate up by the arms.
- "Number 1" and "number 2" players, together form one circle around a group of cones. They hold one another by the hands and each tries to push the other toward the cones.

TOGETHER

OBJECTIVES
Stimulating cohesiveness.
Developing awareness of one's own skills and perception.

EQUIPMENT
One ball per player.

AREA OF PLAY
The penalty area.

PLAYERS
The players are divided into groups of three players and each player is numbered from 1 to 3. They do not have a specific arrangement.

ACTIVITY
The players dribble the ball toward the direction shown by the coach with his arms. Then, the coach calls out, "Form two groups: even numbers on one side, uneven numbers on the other", and the players execute. When the coach calls out "Go", the players re-start dribbling the ball toward the direction shown by the coach. Then, the coach calls out "Number 1 players in a triangle shape", and the number 1 players execute while the others stop. When the coach calls out "Go" again, everybody re-starts dribbling the ball. Then, the coach calls out "Number 2 players in a triangle shape: dribble around but maintain your distances". Then, when the coach calls out "Go", everybody re-starts dribbling the ball.

The exercise goes on with ever changing orders given by the coach: "Number 3 players, get together and do different feints; the other groups must not move"; "All those who feel that they are speedy (or good, strong, handsome, slow, weak, ugly…), get together"; "All those who feel that they are courageous (or hesitating, generous, reserved, tidy, untidy, optimistic, pessimistic, impulsive, easy-going, cheerful, sad…), get together". After executing the different orders, the players always resume dribbling the ball.

THE GAME OF THE NAME

OBJECTIVES

Visualization.
Reflection.

EQUIPMENT

One ball per player.
As many cards as players; on each card, the coach writes the name of one of the participants.

AREA OF PLAY

The penalty area, or a smaller space, depending on the number of participants.

PLAYERS

The players are divided into two groups, A and B.

ACTIVITY

The coach gives each player of group A a card with the name of a player of group B, making sure that the players of group B do not see their names. The two groups are then arranged at a distance of 2-3 yards from one another. When the coach gives the signal, everybody starts dribbling the ball on the field. Players "B" chase players "A" trying to touch them with their hand. When a player "A" is touched, he must show the player "B", who has touched him, his card; if the name on the card is not the name of that player, the latter must continue to look for the card with his name, chasing other "A" players. On the other hand, if the name corresponds, player "B" quickly dribbles the ball toward the coach and shows him his card. The coach whistles for the end of the exercise and gives him one point. Then, the roles are reversed and the exercise is carried out again.

BALANCE

OBJECTIVES

Balance.
Stop and follow.

EQUIPMENT

Several cones.
Three chairs and a ball per team.

AREA OF PLAY

The penalty area.
Cones are scattered in the penalty area.

PLAYERS

The players are divided into three teams, A, B and C.

ACTIVITY

Each team forms a line next to one of the shorter sides of the penalty area. On the other short side, one chair is placed opposite each team. One player per team climbs up on one of the chairs and stands on only one leg. When the coach gives the signal, the first player in line from each team dribbles the ball forward and fetches a cone which he then places on the chair where his teammate is standing. Then, still dribbling, he goes back and, as soon as he is beyond the goal area, passes the ball to the second player in his line. The latter repeats the movements made by his teammate and places a second cone on the chair of his team, then passes the ball to the third player in his line, and so on until there are no more cones. In the meantime, the coach asks the players on the chairs to change the supporting foot every 10-15 seconds. If the player on the chair causes the cones to fall while his teammate is bringing him another cone, his teammate must put back his cone as well as those that have fallen.

If the cones fall from the chair after the teammate has already put his on the chair, the next teammate must put the fallen cones back on the chair.

The exercise finishes when the cones scattered in the penalty area have been collected. The winner is the team with more cones on the chair.

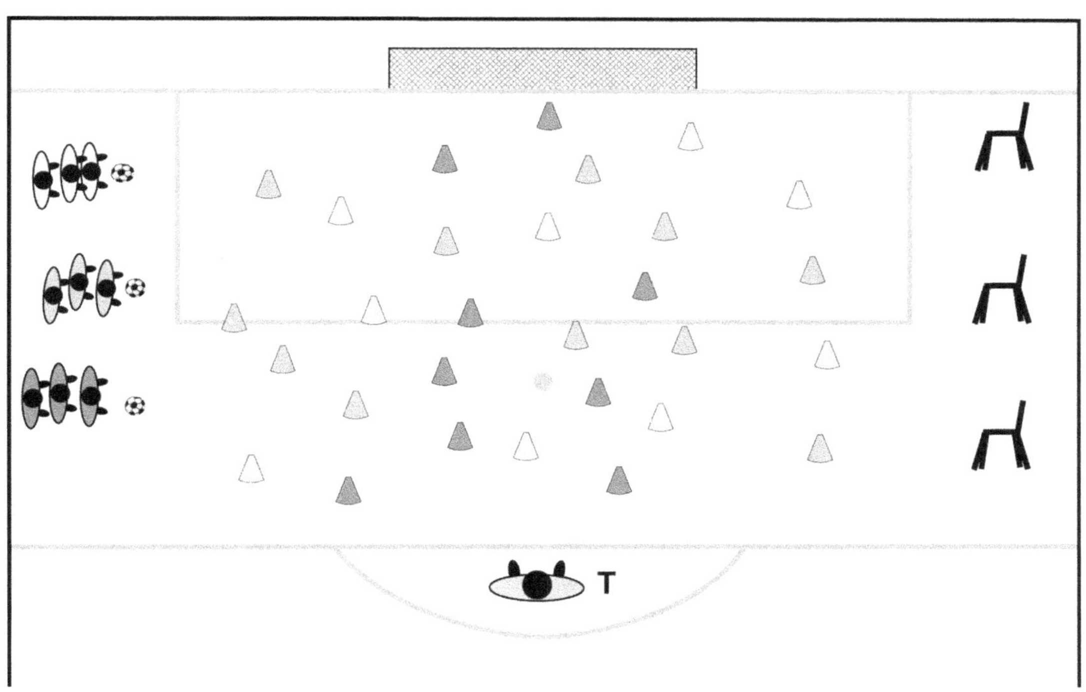

T

CLIPPING THE CLOTHES PINS

OBJECTIVES	Control of the ball. Control of one's own posture. Speed of performance.
EQUIPMENT	One ball per player. Cones, benches or chairs. Several clothes pins: each player should have two.
AREA OF PLAY	The penalty area.
PLAYERS	The players are divided into three teams, A, B and C.
ACTIVITY	One player per team acts as "captain": A1, B1, C1. Each captain places himself on one side of the penalty area, near some cones and two or three benches (the benches are arranged in a row, next to each other; if benches are not available, chairs can be used in the same arrangement). The captains all have an equal number of clothes pins. They must not move. The team is arranged on the field and the coach starts the game. While dribbling the ball, each player must try to clip his clothes pins onto the opponents' shirts, trying not to have clothes pins clipped onto his. When the player has clipped his two clothes pins, he must dribble the ball toward his captain and take two more clothes pins from him. After taking the two clothes pins, the player puts one cone on his head and walks forward and back on the row of benches. After that, he gets off the benches and, while dribbling the ball, tries to clip the two clothes pins on his opponents' shirts. The exercise finishes when one of the captains runs out of clothes pins: his team scores a point. Then the captains are changed and the exercise re-starts. The winner is the team which has scored more points after a pre-established number of goes.

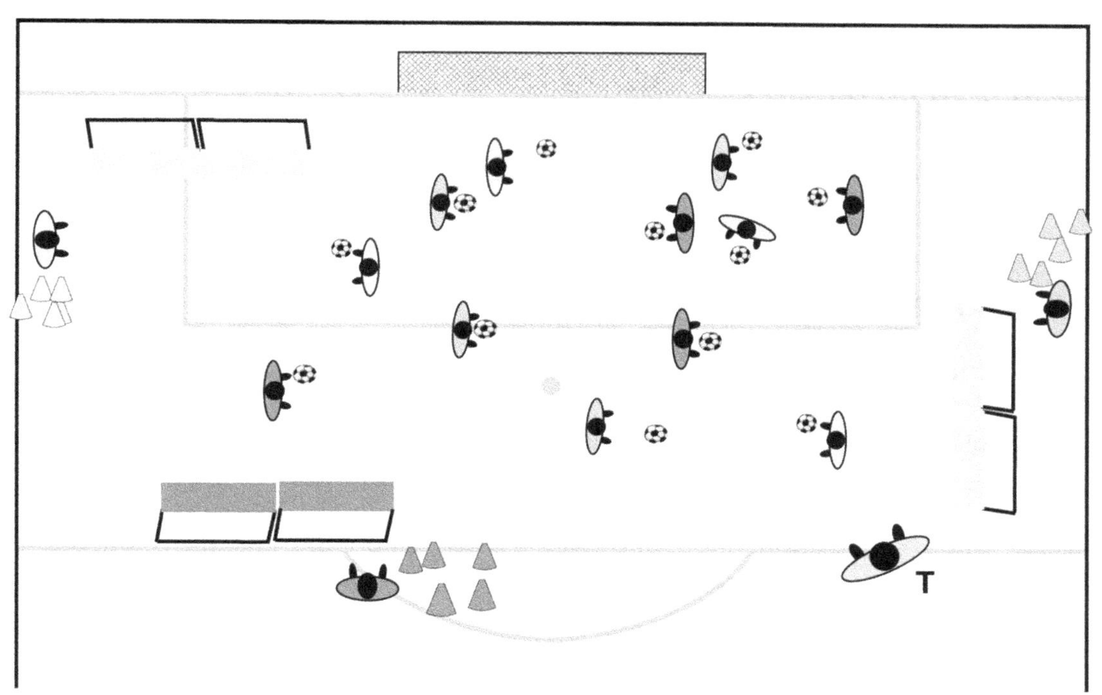

T

USING THE ARMS - ONE

OBJECTIVE

Lateralization.

EQUIPMENT

One ball per player.
A few wooden or cardboard boards.
A few cones.

AREA OF PLAY

The penalty area.

PLAYERS

The players are arranged in a line.

ACTIVITY

1. The players are placed at about 10 yards from the goal area. Inside the goal area, a pyramid-shaped target is made with cones (see diagram). When the coach gives the signal, the first player in line dribbles the ball forward to the long side of the goal area by touching it with only one foot. When he reaches the goal area, he stops the ball with the sole of the foot, picks it up with only one hand and throws it at the target, trying to knock down as many cones as possible. Then, he goes to the back of the line and the second player can start. Each cone knocked down scores one point.
2. A few wooden tiles are arranged in a straight line, at a distance of 3 yards from each other. When the coach gives the signal, the players take turns dribbling the ball by touching it with only one foot (for example, with the left foot) while stepping on the tiles with the other foot (the right one).
3. The coach throws the ball by rolling it forward; the first player in line runs after it and stops it with the sole or with the inside of the foot. Then he goes to the back of the line and the second player can start.

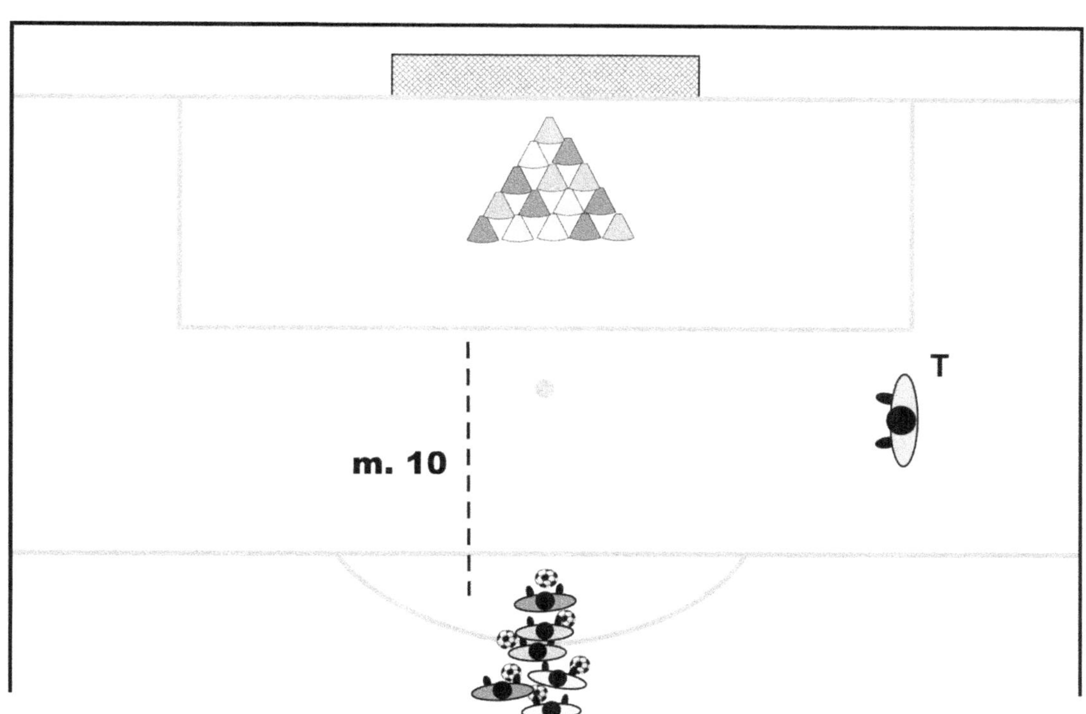

T
m. 10

USING THE ARMS - TWO

OBJECTIVE Lateralization.

EQUIPMENT One ball per player.
A few balloons.
A few cones.
A few of the goals used in 5-a-side soccer.

AREA OF PLAY The penalty area.

PLAYERS The players are either scattered on the field or arranged in a line, as described below.

ACTIVITY 1. Scattered on the field, the players dribble the ball in the direction shown by the coach. When the coach gives the signal, each player picks up his ball, bounces it, throws it or seizes it in one of the following ways:
- like in basketball, he bounces it on the ground;
- he bounces it on various parts of his body; on his forearm, chest, palm of the hand, shoulder, thigh, foot, etc.
- he throws the ball with only one hand, and catches it with only one hand: at chest height, over the shoulder, under the waist.

2. The players are scattered on the field. The balloons are tied to the 5-a-side soccer goals in such a way as to hang at a higher height than the players' heads. The players dribble the ball in the direction shown by the coach, practicing one foot at a time.
When the coach gives the signal, the players dribble the ball toward the balloons, and hit them with their fist.

3. The players are arranged in a line. Along one side of the field, 15 to 20 cones are arranged on their sides about 3 yards apart.
The players are at a distance of about 15 yards from the cones. When the coach gives the signal, the first player in line dribbles the ball forward to the cones, and, with only one hand, puts them upright. The next player knocks them down to their side again, and so on until all the players have done the exercise.

USING THE ARMS - THREE

OBJECTIVE   Lateralization.

EQUIPMENT   A few balls.
One tennis ball.

AREA OF PLAY   The penalty area.

PLAYERS   The players are either arranged in a line or scattered on the field, as described below.

ACTIVITY
1. The players are arranged in a line. The balls are arranged in a line at a distance of about 3 yards from one another. One at a time, the players must run and, using only one foot (either with the inside or the outside of the foot), slightly touch the balls, one after the other, without moving them.
The players should practice one foot at a time.
If any balls are moved, players take turns in putting them back into the line so that the exercise can continue.
2. The players are arranged in a line. The balls are arranged in such a way as to form two parallel lines. One at a time, the players run, and, alternating their feet, touch the balls; the right foot slightly touches the balls on the right, while the left foot slightly touches the balls on the left.
3. The players are scattered on the field. A few players are inside the goal area, while the others are in the penalty area. All of them dribble the ball in the direction shown by the coach, touching the ball with only one foot. One player, called "player A", holds a tennis ball in his hand. When the coach gives the signal, the players stop the ball. Depending on the coach's instructions, player A throws the tennis ball either to the player whose name is called out by the coach, or to the one who is farther away from him or to the one who is closer to him. The player who receives the ball throws it again according to the instructions given by the coach.

CHOOSING THE CAPTAIN

OBJECTIVES

Checking relationships among the players.
Determining the players' ambition.
Changing of direction: about face.

EQUIPMENT

One ball per player.
Five-six cards per player.

AREA OF PLAY

The penalty area.

PLAYERS

The players are scattered on the field.

ACTIVITY

Before the exercise, the coach explains to the players that the cards are "votes" for the player who they intend to choose as their captain. When the coach gives the signal, the players start to dribble the ball and give out or ask for cards. This activity should not last more than 10 seconds. Each player can give out one or more cards, or he can even abstain (keeping his cards and not asking for any). Once the time is over, when the coach gives the "about face" signal, the players go back to the starting point. The player with the highest number of cards scores a point. Then, each player gets back his cards and another repetition is started.

The player who has scored more points at the end of a pre-established number of repetitions becomes the team's captain. The following are some ways to carry out the about face:

1. the player stops the ball with the sole of the foot and, pivoting on the supporting leg, carries out a quick about face movement, moving the ball with the foot with which he has stopped it. Then he dribbles the ball forward toward the new direction with the outside of the foot.

2. The player stops the ball by putting the inside of the foot on the top half of the ball. He immediately carries out an about face movement, by pivoting on the supporting foot. Then he continues to dribble the ball toward the new direction with the foot on which he has pivoted.

DRIBBLING IN PAIRS

OBJECTIVES
Watching.
Cooperating with one's teammate.
Making contact with one's teammate.

EQUIPMENT
One ball per player.
Some plastic tape.

AREA OF PLAY
The goal area.

PLAYERS
The players are arranged in pairs. Some pairs are on one side of the field, the other pairs are on the opposite side.

ACTIVITY
1. The players in each pair are opposite each other and have their hands resting on each other's shoulder; when the coach gives the signal, they dribble the ball forward with the inside or with the outside of the foot, to the opposite side of the field.
2. When the coach gives the signal, the players in each pair join hands and dribble the ball forward to the opposite side of the field.
3. The players are on all fours and are tied in pairs by a piece of plastic tape. When the coach gives the signal, they push the ball forward to the opposite side of the field. During the movement, the ball must be covered with the upper body and must be touched at every step.
4. The players in each pair are back to back, and when the coach gives the signal they join hands. They must dribble the ball to the other side of the field; in each pair, the player who is behind drags the ball either with the sole or with the inside of the foot, alternating the right and the left foot. Then the players in each pair exchange their roles.

ADVICE
The players in each pair should be changed at each exercise.

"SIT BEHIND ME"

OBJECTIVES	Stimulating attention. Control of the ball. Learning one's teammates' names.
EQUIPMENT	One ball per player. Twice as many chairs as the number of players.
AREA OF PLAY	The chairs must be arranged in a line at different distances from one another.
PLAYERS	The players are divided into two five-player teams (team A and team B).
ACTIVITY	All the players of team A and all those of team B alternate in occupying the chairs. The players put their ball under each chair. When the coach gives the signal, player B5 (the last in his line) starts the game by calling player A1 (the first in his line). Player A1 dribbles the ball forward by zigzagging through the chairs. While he is dribbling the ball forward, team B players try to tackle him with their feet (they can move their legs and body from the chair for this purpose, however, they are not allowed to take their hands off the chair); player A1 must be careful not to let them touch his ball. Then he sits behind player B5 and calls player B1, who is the first in team B's line. The exercise goes on like this, with the player who is the last in his line calling the opponent who is first in the opposing team's line, who after dribbling the ball as described above sits behind him. The player who manages to dribble the ball without letting the opponents touch it scores one point for his team.
ADVICE	If the number of players is uneven, the coach sits at the end of the line and starts the game by calling the first of the line in the other team.

BALL INTO THE GOAL

OBJECTIVES

Watching the opponent.
Attention and reaction.

EQUIPMENT

One ball per player.
A few cones.

AREA OF PLAY

The penalty area.
A few 7-8-yard-wide goals are formed on the sides of the penalty area by using cones; with other cones, another area is marked about 3 yards away from the penalty area.

PLAYERS

The players are divided into two teams (teams A and B)
In each team, the players are numbered sequentially.

ACTIVITY

Team A is arranged in the goal area while team B is arranged in the area marked with the cones. When the coach gives the signal, all the players start dribbling the ball in their area. When the coach gives the "about face" signal, all the players do an about face and keep on dribbling the ball without restrictions. Then the coach calls out a number, for example "3". Team B's player 3 tries to take the ball into one of the goals, while team A's player 3 chases him to prevent him from doing so. The other players stop. Team B's player has a prescribed amount of time to take the ball into one of the goals, and this time is counted aloud by the coach. If team A's player 3 manages to steal the ball, the contest continues and team B's player 3 must try to steal the ball back while the former controls the ball and tries to keep possession till the time has expired. A point is scored by a player when he manages to take the ball into one of the goals; if he does not, the point is scored by the opponents. Two halves are played; at the end of the first half, the teams exchange roles.

ADVICE

1. The skills of the players with the same number on each team should be comparable.
2. The player who dribbles the ball should be required to start at maximum speed, dribbling the ball forward with long kicks; in addition, he should be required to slow down if the opponent reaches him (so that the opponent slows down too), and to then accelerate and beat the opponent.
3. The "chasers" should be reminded to be ready to start immediately.

SNOW BALL FIGHT

OBJECTIVES

Overcoming shyness.
Being aggressive in a cheerful way.
Controlling the ball.

EQUIPMENT

One ball per player.
Newspapers to make paper "snow balls".

AREA OF PLAY

The penalty area, or any other not too large space suitable to the number of players, where some "snow balls" are scattered (other "snow balls" are laid next to the coach). A few work stations to practice different skills are prepared outside the area of play.

PLAYERS

The players are scattered on the field.

ACTIVITY

When the coach gives the signal, the players dribble the ball around the field without restriction. Then the coach says "it's snowing" and throws the paper "snow balls" onto the field, one after another. Then he says "prevent the ball from touching the snow". The penalty for the player whose ball touches one of the paper "snow balls" is to stop for a few seconds. When the "snowfall" is over, the coach says "look for a teammate and start a snow fight with him". Then, still dribbling, the players pick up the "snow balls" to throw them at each other. The players must keep the sole of the foot on the ball when they pick up the "snow ball" and when they throw the "snow ball" at each other. If a player fails to do this, he must get off the playing field and do some exercises at a work station for a few minutes. The "snow fight" is a timed game; at the end of the prescribed time, each player must look for another teammate with whom to start another "snow fight".

FREEING TOUCH

OBJECTIVE

Cooperating even while competing with each other.

EQUIPMENT

One ball per player.

AREA OF PLAY

The penalty area, or any other space which is big enough for the number of players.

PLAYERS

The players are divided into three to four-player groups (or even larger groups).

ACTIVITY

The players of the various groups are scattered on the field, except for one player, player A, who at first is placed outside the field and has to act as a "chaser", while the others dribble the ball around the field. Those who are touched by the "chaser" stop and, with the sole of the right foot, make the ball roll from the right to the left; then, with a hop, they move to the right and, with the

sole

of the left foot, make the ball roll from the left to the right. They do this until a teammate from their group touches their back and "frees" them. The "chaser" has a prescribed time (3 minutes) to stop and prevent the other players from being freed.

The game finishes when all the players have acted as "chasers".

The winner is the player who manages to stop the highest number of players.

MUSICALLY - ONE

OBJECTIVES

Overcoming shyness.
Dribbling the ball quickly.
Turning around.

EQUIPMENT

One ball per player.

AREA OF PLAY

A space suitable to the game.

PLAYERS

The players are divided into two teams (team A and team B); they are arranged in a line, sitting on the ground, facing forward (looking at the back of the player in front of them), with their arms crossed on their chest, and each of them has his ball between his thighs.
The players on each team are numbered sequentially.

ACTIVITY

When the coach gives the signal, the players start to sing, unfold their arms, and drum with their hands on the back of their teammate who is sitting in front of them. As the coach calls out a number, the two players (one in team A and the other in team B) with that number, get up, quickly dribble the ball around their team and get back to the starting point. The player who is the first to return to the starting point scores a point for his team.

ADVICE

1. The players with the same numbers should have comparable skills.
2. The players should circle the line of their teammates as follows: They should approach the ball with a quick forward movement to the left of the left foot (as if they were to make a pass with the right foot) and when the outside of the right foot reaches the ball, they should pivot on the right foot and, with a close control, restart dribbling it with the left foot. To turn to the left, the player's movement would be the reverse of that described above.

INSIDE/OUTSIDE - ONE

OBJECTIVES

Control of the ball.
Perception of space in a fixed situation.

EQUIPMENT

Several empty plastic bottles.
A few poles.

AREA OF PLAY

The penalty area.
The poles are used to build one enclosure per team; an even number of bottles is placed inside each enclosure.

PLAYERS

The players are divided into three to four-player teams.

ACTIVITY

The players of each team are arranged opposite each other outside the enclosure that their team has been assigned. When the coach gives the "inside and outside" signal, all the players dribble the ball into the enclosure and then out of it, trying to avoid knocking down the plastic bottles. After a prescribed period of time (2 or 3 minutes), the coach stops the game.
One point is scored by the team which has knocked down the fewest bottles at the end of the repetition.

ADVICE

Each team should have approximately the same number of players in each skill level.

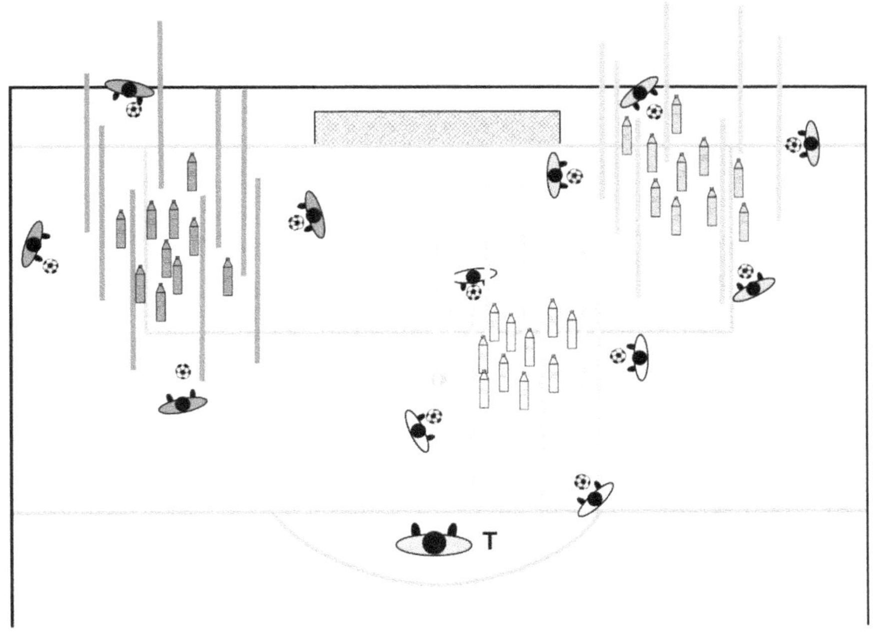

DRIBBLING TO GOAL IN A ZIG-ZAG

OBJECTIVES

Quickness of reflex.
Dribbling the ball around a circle.

EQUIPMENT

One ball per player.
A few poles.

AREA OF PLAY

Two circles marked by cones 3 yards apart

PLAYERS

The players are divided into two teams (team A and team B).
The players of each team are numbered sequentially.

ACTIVITY

The players of each team place themselves inside the team's circle. They start dribbling the ball in the direction shown by the coach; then, the coach calls out a number (for example, "1"). The players corresponding to that number (one player in team A and one player in team B) start dribbling the ball by slaloming through the cones, until they get back to the starting point; once they are back to the starting point, they lay that cone on its side. The other players stay put.
This exercise should be repeated several times.

ADVICE

The players with the same numbers should have comparable skills.

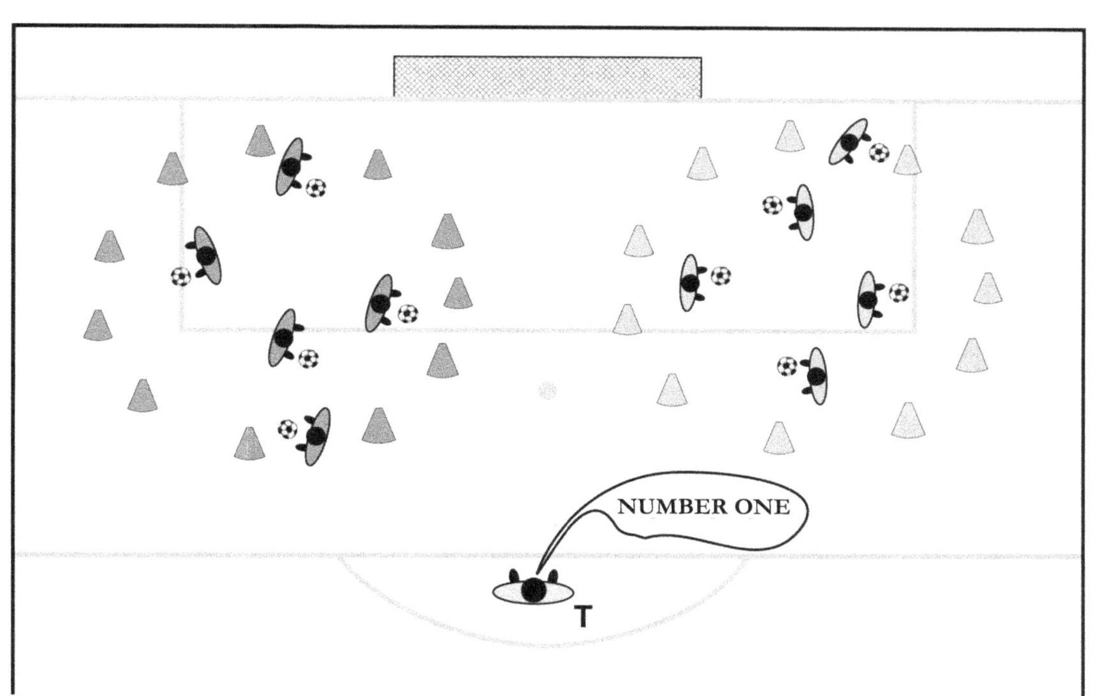

NUMBER ONE
T

THROWING THE BALL

OBJECTIVES

Dribbling the ball quickly.
Lateralization.

EQUIPMENT

One ball per player, plus one ball for the coach.

AREA OF PLAY

An area suitable to the number of players involved.

PLAYERS

The players are arranged in a wide circle.

ACTIVITY

The coach places himself in the middle of the wide circle formed by the players, with the ball in his hands. He starts the game by throwing the ball up in the air and calling the name of one player, perhaps player "A". Player A rushes to catch the ball, and the other players try to quickly move away from him while dribbling their ball. Once player A has caught the ball, he calls out "stop". The other players stop, and player A tries to hit one of them by throwing the ball with only one hand or by kicking it with the instep (player A is allowed to take three steps before throwing the ball with his hand).
If player A hits a player, he scores a point; otherwise, the coach restarts the game and calls player A again until he manages to hit the target. After each throw, both player A and the others go back to their initial position.
This exercise should be repeated several times.

ADVICE

1. Alternate the arms when throwing the ball.
2. The coach should require the players dribbling the ball to touch it also with the instep (with the laces). The supporting foot in this case is outstretched.

"WATCH CAREFULLY"

OBJECTIVES

Control of the ball.
Visual attention.

EQUIPMENT

One ball per player.

AREA OF PLAY

An area suitable to the number of players involved.

PLAYERS

The players are divided into two teams (teams A and B)

ACTIVITY

The coach asks the players on team A to carefully observe team B's players for a few seconds, counted aloud by the coach. Then, team A's players turn their backs to team B and team B moves away. Once team B is away, one of its players changes something in his clothes (some examples: he lowers or raises one sock, fastens a clothes pin or a small card on his shorts or shirt, wears his shirt or shorts inside out, exchanges his shirt with a teammate, wears his shirt with the number in the front, puts a small plastic tape into his shorts and lets a small part hang out from the back, wears his shirt, or part of it, outside his shorts, etc.). Then, the coach gives the signal and the teams dribble the ball around the field. The aim of team B is to dribble the ball away from team A, without letting their opponents spot the change. The aim of team A is to dribble the ball toward the players of team B in order to find out which opponent has changed something in his clothes and how. A point is scored by team A when one of its players calls out both the name of the player on team B who has changed something and what he has changed.

When the prescribed time for the each repetition is over, the teams exchange roles. The number of repetitions should correspond to the number of players on each team, so that every player on a team has the opportunity to play the role of the "modified" player.

VARIATION

OBJECTIVE

Cooperating even while competing with each other.

ACTIVITY

Each player takes a turn to find out who has changed something. He dribbles the ball among the other players to find the player who has modified his clothes.
He has a prescribed period of time to discover who has modified something and what he has modified.

INSIDE/OUTSIDE - TWO

OBJECTIVES

Paying attention.
Finding one's bearings.

EQUIPMENT

One ball per player.
Poles and chairs.
Pieces of plastic tape.

AREA OF PLAY

The penalty area.
The poles and the chairs are used to build small
enclosures for each pair of players.

PLAYERS

The players are divided into pairs.

ACTIVITY

1. When the coach yells "everybody inside", maintaining
   their pairing, each player dribbles his ball into the
   enclosure; when the coach yells "everybody outside",
   once again, while maintaining their pairing, each player
   dribbles his ball out of the enclosure. When the coach
   signals "everybody inside (or outside), counterclockwise around", maintaining their pairing, each player
   dribbles the ball counterclockwise around the enclosure
   inside or outside, as directed by the coach. When the
   coach gives the signal "everybody zigzag", again maintaining their pairing, each player dribbles the ball
   through the poles that mark the circle of the enclosure.
   And so on.
2. One player in each pair places himself in the middle of
   the enclosure; the other player (player B) remains
   outside with the ball, opposite his teammate. Player A
   makes a sign to player B meaning "inside", and then
   player B dribbles the ball into the enclosure. Player A
   can make other signs, such as "outside", "zigzag",
   "inside and outside", etc. Player B must always carry
   out his teammate's orders.
3. Like point 2 above, but this time player B carries out
   movements contrary to player A's orders.
4. One player in each pair, player B, is outside the
   enclosure opposite his teammate and takes one piece of
   plastic tape and puts into his shorts, letting it hang out
   like a tail. Both players in each pair are dribbling a ball.
   While dribbling the ball, player B changes directions
   suddenly (counterclockwise-clockwise, inside-outside
   the enclosure); player A follows him while dribbling his
   ball, trying to catch his "tail". When he succeeds, they
   exchange roles.

INSIDE/OUTSIDE - THREE

OBJECTIVES

Balance.
Dribbling the ball quickly.

EQUIPMENT

Poles and chairs.

AREA OF PLAY

The penalty area.
On one end of the field, the poles are used to build one enclosure per player.
One chair per player, with each chair placed inside each player's enclosure.
On the opposite end, a few cones are arranged in a row.

PLAYERS

The players are divided into two teams (teams A and B).

ACTIVITY

The players of two teams are behind the row of cones, and they each dribble the ball in the direction shown by the coach. When the coach gives the signal "into the enclosures", each player must dribble his ball into his enclosure, get on his chair and, standing on only one foot, throw the ball upward and then catch it. Each player must maintain his balance for a prescribed length of time. The player who loses his balance must get off his chair, quickly dribble the ball back toward the starting point, turn around one cone and go back to his chair to try again. Once the prescribed amount of time has expired, the coach calls out "outside the enclosures". At that moment, he counts how many players in each team are still balanced on their chairs. The team with more players still balanced on their chairs gets one point.

ADVICE

1. After each repetition, the players should be required to alternate the leg they use to stand on their chair.
2. When the players dribble the ball quickly, the coach should require them to touch it also with the instep.

INSIDE/OUTSIDE - FOUR

OBJECTIVES

Speed of performance.
Lateralization.
Control of the ball in a fixed situation.

EQUIPMENT

Two bags filled with any kind of object, for example socks, shirts, shoes, plastic glasses, tennis balls.

AREA OF PLAY

The penalty area.
One circuit per team is made by using small "enclosures" arranged in a zigzagging way, at a distance of 3-4 yards from one another.
On one end of each circuit, there is a bag full of objects. The enclosures are built with poles and chairs, and a few cones are placed inside them to make the dribbling of the ball more difficult.

PLAYERS

The players are divided into two teams (teams A and B). The players on each team are numbered sequentially.

ACTIVITY

The players of each team are arranged in a line in front of the starting point of their circuit. When the coach calls out a number, the players with that number begin the circuit and dribble the ball through the enclosures as far as the bag at the end. When they reach the bag, they take out all the objects in it with only one hand, then put all the objects back into it, still using only one hand. Finally, they dribble the ball back to the starting point. The player who is the first to finish the circuit scores a point for his team.

ADVICE

1. The players should alternate their hands in emptying and filling the bag.
2. The players with the same numbers should have comparable skills.

INSIDE/OUTSIDE - FIVE

OBJECTIVES	Dribbling the ball quickly. Stopping the ball.
EQUIPMENT	One ball per player. Several pieces of plastic tape. A few cones.
AREA OF PLAY	The penalty area. On one end of the area of play, the cones are used to form a number of small squares, the number corresponding to the number of players minus one.
PLAYERS	The players are divided into two teams (teams A and B).
ACTIVITY	Starting from the end of the area of play opposite to where the squares have been laid out, the players, in a random arrangement, dribble their ball in the direction shown by the coach. When the coach gives the signal "inside", each player dribbles his ball as quickly as he can, trying to avoid being the last player to get into a square. Since the number of squares is one less than the number of players, one player will not be able to find a square that is not already occupied. He remains out and must hang a piece of plastic tape from his shorts to show his penalty. When the coach gives the signal "outside", all the players return to the starting point and the exercise restarts. The exercise goes on like this for a prescribed number of times. At the end, the coach counts the number of pieces of plastic tape in the players' shorts. The team with the smallest number is the winner.

INSIDE/OUTSIDE - SIX

OBJECTIVES

Spine mobility.
Finding one's bearings.

EQUIPMENT

One ball per player.
Poles, chairs and cones.
Pieces of plastic tape.

AREA OF PLAY

The penalty area.
One enclosure per pair is built by using the poles and the chairs.

PLAYERS

The players are divided into pairs.

ACTIVITY

1. The players of each pair are on all fours opposite each other, outside the enclosure. One player in each pair ("player A") puts a piece of plastic tape into his shorts and lets it hang out like a tail. When the coach gives the signal, all the pairs enter the enclosure with each player while pushing his ball forward on all fours, covering it with his upper body. Player B tries to pull the tail away from his partner; when he succeeds, the players exchange roles.
2. The pairs push the ball forward on all fours in the part of the field which is opposite to where the enclosures are built. When the coach gives the signal, each pair moves into one of the enclosures with each of the two players pushing the ball forward on all fours. The pair that reaches one of the enclosures first puts one piece of plastic tape into their shorts. After a prescribed number of repetitions, the winner is the pair that has more pieces of plastic tape.
3. A few cones are put into the enclosures.
   When the coach gives the signal "everybody inside", each player in each pair pushes the ball forward into the enclosure on all fours, while covering it with his upper body. When the coach gives the signal "every body zigzag", each player pushes the ball forward through the poles on all fours, and so on. The cones are used to make the exercise more difficult.

4. In the middle of the enclosure there is a cone laid on
   its side. According to the instruction given by the
   coach, the players move on all fours and go:
   - outside the enclosure, to the right or to the left of
     the cone;
   - inside the enclosure, to the right or to the left of the
     cone;
   - inside the enclosure, behind or in front of the
     cone;
   - outside the enclosure, behind or in front of the
     cone.

RIGHT/LEFT - ONE

OBJECTIVE	Finding one's bearings.
EQUIPMENT	One ball per player. A few poles.
AREA OF PLAY	The penalty area.
PLAYERS	The players are scattered opposite the coach.

ACTIVITY

1. One cone, lying on its side, is placed in front of each player. The coach asks the players to:
   - dribble the ball to the cone in front of them and dribble it back;
   - dribble the ball to the right and then to the left of the cone in front of them.

   During the exercise, the coach changes his position every now and then, moving to another part of the field.

2. A line of cones is placed in front of each player. The coach asks the players to dribble the ball:
   - to the right of the cones, while stretching their right arm toward the right side of the field;
   - to the left of the cones, while stretching their left arm toward the left side of the field;
   - to the left of the cones, while stretching their left arm toward the right side of the field.

3. One cone, lying on its side, is placed in front of each player. The coach asks the players to dribble the ball:
   - to the right and then to the left of the cone in front of them, while stretching out their right or left arm;
   - toward the cone and then back, while keeping their arms stretched forward or back and low.

During the exercise, the coach changes his position every now and then.

"PULL THE TAIL AWAY" - TWO

OBJECTIVES

Control of the ball.
Quickness of reflex.
Getting organized in a line.

EQUIPMENT

One ball and a piece of plastic tape per player.

AREA OF PLAY

The penalty area, or any other area suitable to the number of players involved.

PLAYERS

The players are arranged in a line.

ACTIVITY

Each player puts a piece of plastic tape into the back of his shorts, letting it hang out like a tail. Then, all the players except one (player A) arrange themselves in a line behind the coach. Player A sits behind the goal, without the ball. The coach gives the signal and the players start dribbling the ball in a line, following the coach in his movements. When the coach calls out "pull the tailaway" the players break out of the line formation and try to dribble their balls off the field before player A, running after them, can pull the tail away from a dribbling player. Player A scores one point for every tail that he pulls away. The game continues with another player who acts as "player A".

The game finishes when each player has acted as "player A" for a prescribed number of times.

"SCORE MANY GOALS"

OBJECTIVES

Control of the ball.
Quickness of performance.
Shooting at goal.

EQUIPMENT

Several balls and cones.
Two small goals.

AREA OF PLAY

The penalty area.
The cones are used to extend the longer side of the goal area as far as it meets the short sides of the penalty area, thus marking two zones.
About 10 yards from the cones, a small goal is placed inside each zone (see diagram below).

PLAYERS

The players are divided into two teams.

ACTIVITY

Each team is arranged inside one of the two zones and behind the small goal within that zone. Opposite each team, beyond the cones, an equal number of balls is placed for each team. When the coach gives the signal, each player sprints and gets a ball and starts dribbling it back. On their way back, as soon as a player passes the cones, he shoots at the small goal in his zone and then gets another ball, repeating the exercise. When a team has used up all its balls, the game is over. A point is scored by the team with the higher number of balls inside its goal.

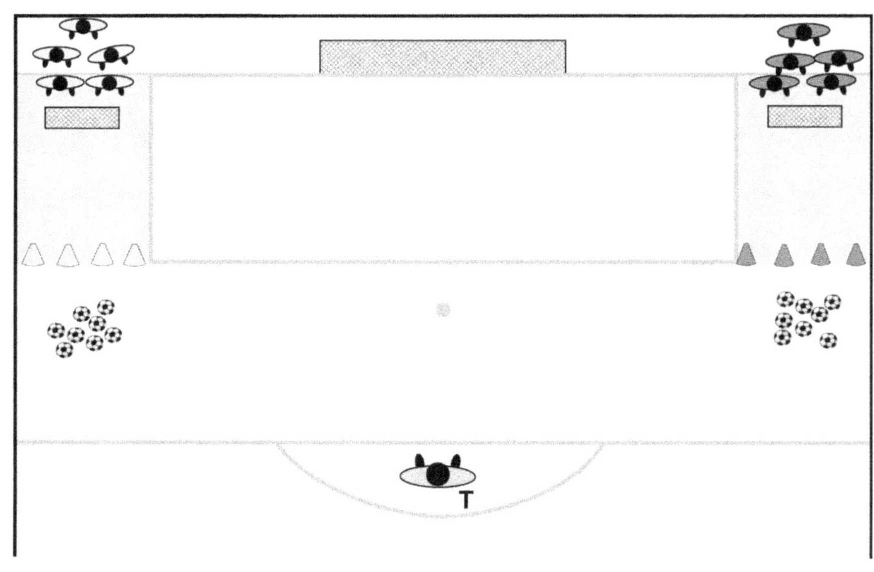

ZIGZAGGING

OBJECTIVES

Finding one's bearings.
Changing direction.
Watching.
Touching the ball with purpose.

EQUIPMENT

One ball per player.
A few cones.

AREA OF PLAY

The penalty area.

PLAYERS

The players are scattered on the field, opposite the coach.

ACTIVITY

1. A line of 6-8 cones about 3 yards apart is placed in front of each player. The coach asks the players to:
   - dribble the ball straight ahead to the right of the cones, changing direction once, near a cone that the coach specifies during the player's dribble (for example, the second one or the third one);
   - dribble the ball straight ahead to the right of the cones, changing direction two or more times every two or three cones;
   - dribble the ball through the cones, changing direction one or more times.
2. Two parallel lines of cones about 12-16 inches apart are placed in front of each player. The coach asks the players to:
   - dribble the ball through the cones, changing direction only once;
   - dribble the ball through the cones, changing direction frequently.
3. Two lines of cones 1 yard apart are placed in front of each player. Each player dribbles the ball starting, for example, from the first cone in the line on his right toward the first cone in the line on his left, then toward the second cone in the line on his left, then toward the second cone in the line on his right, then toward the third cone in the line on his right, and so on.

CLEARING THE FIELD - ONE

OBJECTIVES

Control of the ball.
Dribbling the ball in a difficult situation.
Watching.

EQUIPMENT

Different objects to drag (bags, chairs, old tires) tied to a rope so that they can be dragged.
A few poles and cones.

AREA OF PLAY

The penalty area.
The cones are used to divide the penalty area into two halves; in each half, a number of poles (which is the same for both teams) is driven into the ground, and next to each pole there is an object to drag.

PLAYERS

The players are divided into two teams: teams A and B.

ACTIVITY

Each team is arranged in one of the two halves of the area of play. When the coach gives the signal, each player dribbles the ball with pace toward the opposing half of the area of play, dragging the objects from his half of the penalty area to the opponents' half. While he is dribbling the ball, he heads for those poles in the opponents' half of the penalty area which no longer have objects at their base because a player has already dragged them. When he arrives at one of these poles, he leaves the object he dragged next to it.
The exercise lasts one or two minutes, according to the players' skills.
One point is scored by the team that has dragged more objects into the opponents' half of the penalty area at the end of the prescribed time.

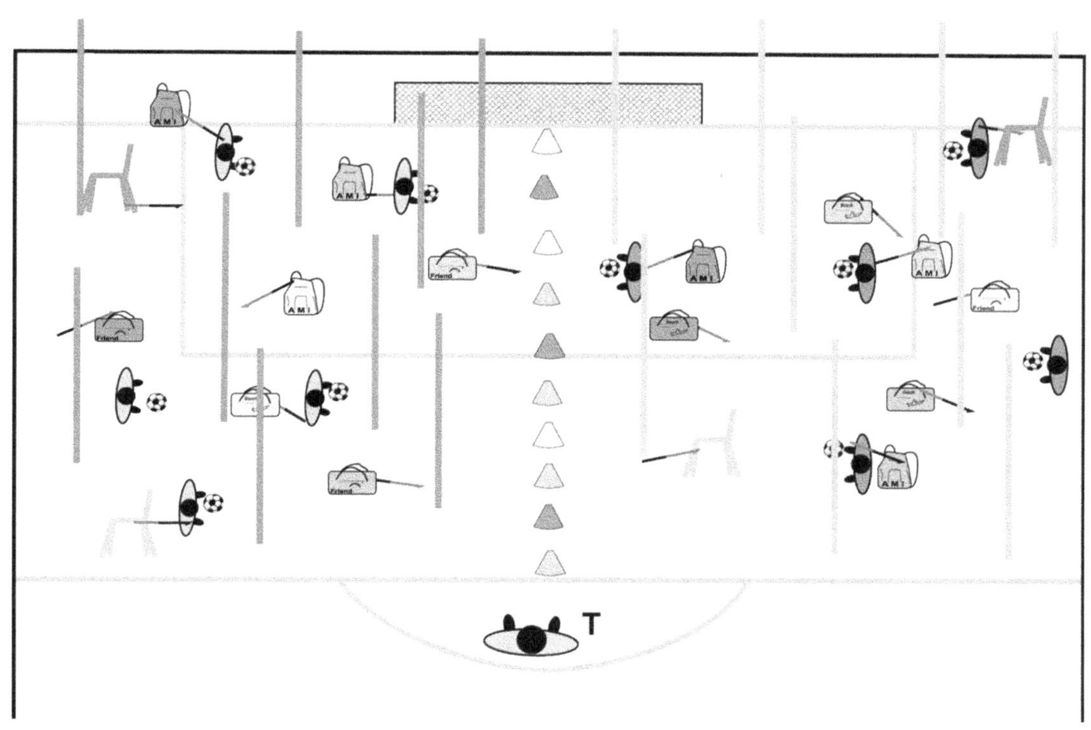

"GO TO THE BASE"

OBJECTIVE

Dribbling at speed.

EQUIPMENT

One ball per player.
A few pieces of plastic tape.

AREA OF PLAY

It is made up of four bases arranged in a circle about 15 yards apart, and at the center of the circle there is a fifth base.

PLAYERS

The players are divided into four groups: A, B, C and D.

ACTIVITY

Each group of players is arranged in one of the four bases. The coach calls out one group, and that group must quickly dribble the ball into the base in the center of the circle, where there are no players. The player of the dribbling group who is the last to get into the central base has to put a piece of plastic tape into his shorts, and let it hang out like a tail. The winner is the player who, after a prescribed number of repetitions, has fewer pieces of plastic tape in his shorts.

ADVICE

The players in each group should have the same skill levels.

"DRIBBLE MORE BALLS"

OBJECTIVE   Spine mobility.

EQUIPMENT   Several balls.

AREA OF PLAY   The goal area.
Each of the four corners of the goal area is a "zone", and is occupied by one team.
The balls are scattered in the goal area.

PLAYERS   The players are divided into four teams: A, B, C and D.
The players on each team are numbered sequentially.

ACTIVITY   Each of the four teams is assigned one of the four zones. The players are arranged in their zone, on all fours. When the coach gives the signal, the player whose number is 1 in each team moves fast on all fours to reach a ball. Then, still on all fours, he pushes the ball into his team's zone. As soon as he reaches his team's zone, player 2 starts and so on. When there are no more balls on the field, each team counts how many it has managed to collect in its own zone. One point is scored by the team which has collected the greatest number of balls.

FINDING YOUR BEARINGS - FOUR

OBJECTIVES

Dribbling the ball in "forced" spaces.
Control of the ball.
Waiting one's turn.

EQUIPMENT

One ball per player.
A few plastic bottles, poles and cones.

AREA OF PLAY

A space suitable to the exercise.

PLAYERS

The players are divided into two groups (A and B) or into pairs.

ACTIVITY

1. The players are divided into two groups (group A and group B). The poles are laid on the ground on their side to form two parallel lines marking a 12-inch wide path. Group A and group B are arranged at opposite ends of the path. When the coach gives the signal, the players of group A dribble the ball along the path to the opposite end. Then, once they have finished, the players of group B do the same.
2. The players are divided into pairs. The pairs are lined up. The poles are laid on the ground on their side to form two parallel lines marking a 20-inch wide path. Down the center of the path is a line of cones 3 yards apart. When the coach gives the signal, each player in a pair dribbles his ball through the cones from the beginning of the path to the end, trying to get past each cone by touching the ball only once.
3. The players are divided into two groups (group A and group B). The poles are laid on the ground on their side to form two parallel lines marking a 20-inch wide path. Down the center of the path is a line of empty plastic bottles 3 yards apart. Group A is placed at one end of the path and group B is placed at the opposite end. When the coach gives the signal, the first player in each group dribbles the ball weaving through the bottles with his right foot only, paying attention not to knock down the bottles. When the two players meet, each player stops his ball with the sole of the foot or with the inside of the foot and they greet each other by giving each other a high five. They continue to dribble the ball with their left foot to the end of the path; when they reach the end, they line up and wait for their next turn while another two players start.

MAD ROPE - ONE

OBJECTIVES

Watching.
Control of the ball.
Quickness of reflex.

EQUIPMENT

A 7-8-yard long rope.
One ball per player.
A few pieces of plastic tape.

AREA OF PLAY

The penalty area, or any other not too large space suitable
to the exercise.

PLAYERS

The players are divided into two teams (A and B).

ACTIVITY

The players are scattered on the area of play. The coach is
in the middle of the area and holds a rope in his hand.
When he gives the signal, the players dribble the ball
around the field while the coach moves his arm in various
ways so that the rope moves in different directions. The
players who are touched by the rope have to put a piece
of plastic tape into their shorts and let it hang out like a
tail. The game is won by the team with the lowest number
of tails at the end of the prescribed number of
repetitions.

"LOOK UP"

OBJECTIVES

Finding one's bearings.
Paying attention.

EQUIPMENT

One ball per player.
Various objects: poles, cones, bags, chairs, etc.
Cards numbered from 0 to 20.
Four instruments that make four different sounds, for example, a whistle, a tambourine, a little bell and a toy trumpet.

AREA OF PLAY

The penalty area.

PLAYERS

The players are scattered on the field or are grouped.

ACTIVITY

1. A few poles, cones, bags and chairs are placed on different parts of the field. The coach holds the four instruments in his hands.
   The players start from the middle of the area of play and dribble the ball in a different direction depending on the instrument played by the coach, for example:
   - when he blows the whistle, they dribble the ball toward the bags;
   - when he plays the tambourine, they dribble the ball toward the poles;
   - when he plays the toy trumpet, they dribble the ball toward the cones;
   - when he plays the little bell, they dribble the ball toward the chairs.

2. The players dribble the ball in the direction shown by the coach; when he squats, the players turn and dribble the ball toward rectangular areas (outlined by four posts) which are behind them, with a few cones placed inside the areas. The total number of cones is always one less than the number of players still competing. Each rectangular area must be occupied by the same number of players as the number of cones inside the area. The player who cannot find an available space place inside a rectangle is eliminated from the next repetition.

3. The players are divided into groups. Cards numbered 0 to 20 are attached to the chairs with adhesive tape. The chairs are arranged in such a way as to form a circuit. The players take turns dribbling the ball forward by weaving between the chairs, from chair 0 to chair 20.

72

RIGHT/LEFT - TWO

OBJECTIVES

Finding one's bearings.
Organizing the space.

EQUIPMENT

One ball per player.
A few cones.

AREA OF PLAY

A space suitable to the exercise.

PLAYERS

The players are divided into three to four-player groups
(or even in groups with a higher number of players).

ACTIVITY

right

1. Each group is opposite a line of 4 or 5 cones. Again
and again, the coach has the players in each group
weave through the cones dribbling the ball "to the
of the first cone", "to the left of the second cone", "to
the right of the third cone", "to the left of the fourth
cone", and so forth.
2. Each group is opposite a line of 4-5 cones 3 yds apart.
The coach has the players in each group dribble the
ball around each cone, either clockwise or counter
clockwise.
3. The players on each group are numbered sequentially.
All the players are arranged in groups, in a circle, at a
distance of 5-6 yards from each other. The coach and a
player (player "A") are at the center of the circle. The
coach calls out some numbers; each group's player who
has been assigned the number which has been called
out dribbles his ball to the right or to the left in an
attempt to get to another group and exchange places
with a player with the same number who is trying to do
the same. While the players with the called number are
doing their dribbling and trying to get to a vacated
position in a group, player "A" dribbles his ball away
from his position in the center and also tries to reach
one of the temporarily vacated places in a group before
another player gets there. A player who cannot find a
group which has not already been completed joins the
coach in the center.

Every now and then the positions of the groups on the
field should be exchanged.

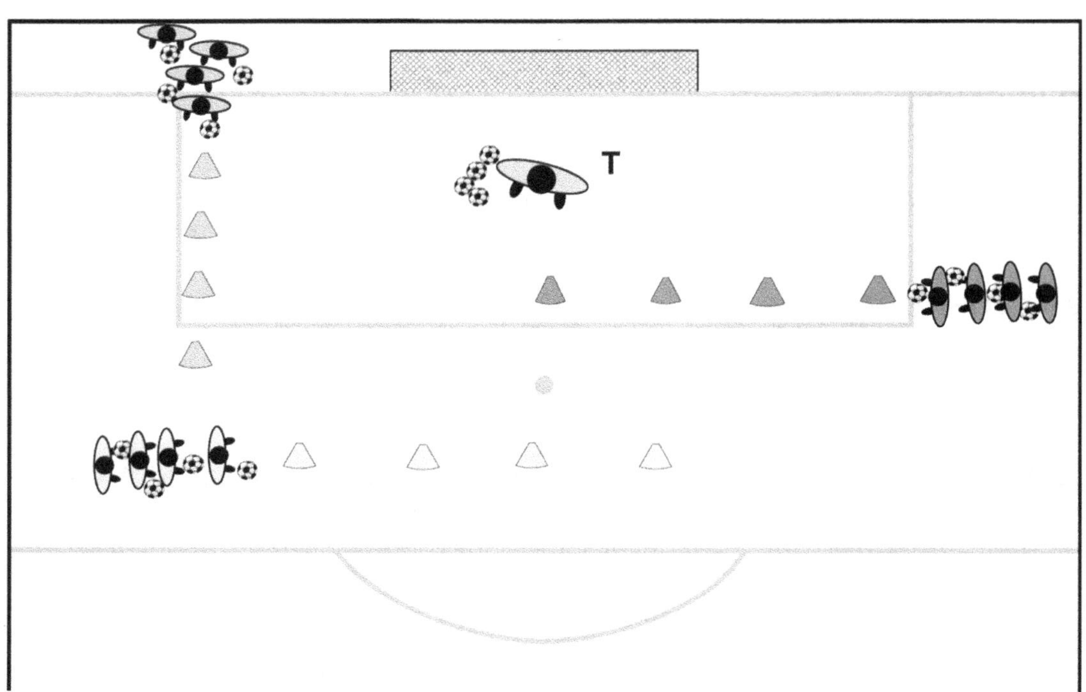

T

HAT STEALER

OBJECTIVES

Dribbling the ball.
Watching.
Speed of performance.

EQUIPMENT

One ball per player.
A few markers, poles and cones.

AREA OF PLAY

The penalty area.
The penalty area is divided into two areas of play by a line of poles. An equal number of cones is scattered in each of the two areas, and on top of each cone a marker is placed as if it were a kind of hat.

PLAYERS

The players are divided into two teams (teams A and B).

ACTIVITY

Each team is given an area of play.
The players are arranged behind the cones.
When the coach gives the signal, every player quickly dribbles the ball into the opposing team's area and steals one "hat" from one of the cones. Then, he dribbles the ball back to his area and puts the "hat" on one of the cones in his area. Then he dribbles the ball back into the opposing team's area to steal another "hat", and keeps repeating this.
Each round continues for a prescribed amount of time (one or two minutes).
One point is scored by the team that, at the end of the round, has stolen the larger number of "hats".

ADVICE

1. Between rounds, the players should carry out breathing exercises.
2. In order to improve the players' ball control, the area of play should not be too large and the cones should be quite close and at varying distances from one another.

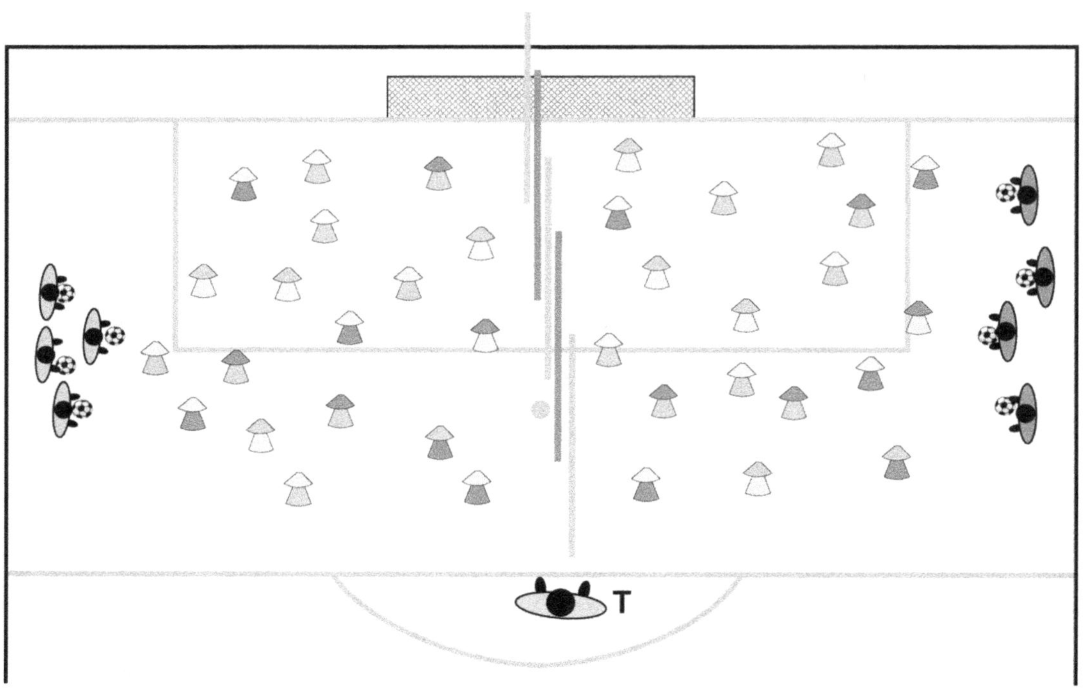

T

"GO AND COME"

OBJECTIVES	Speed of performance. Organizing one's actions.
EQUIPMENT	One ball per player. Four small posts, two chairs and some plastic tape.
AREA OF PLAY	The penalty area. Four small posts are put up in the middle of the penalty area to form two small goals. The goals are about 5-6 yards from each other and in each goal there is a chair. A few pieces of plastic tape are scattered in the penalty area at varying distances from one another.
PLAYERS	The players are divided into two teams.
ACTIVITY	Each team is assigned one of the goals. The chairs are both the starting and the finishing point. When the coach gives the signal, each player starts dribbling the ball and picks up any of the pieces of plastic tape. Then he dribbles the ball back into his goal and puts the plastic tape on the chair. After that, he repeats the exercise. The game finishes when there are no more pieces of plastic tape left on the ground. The team with the highest number of pieces of plastic tape on its chair is the winner. The exercise should be repeated for several repetitions.

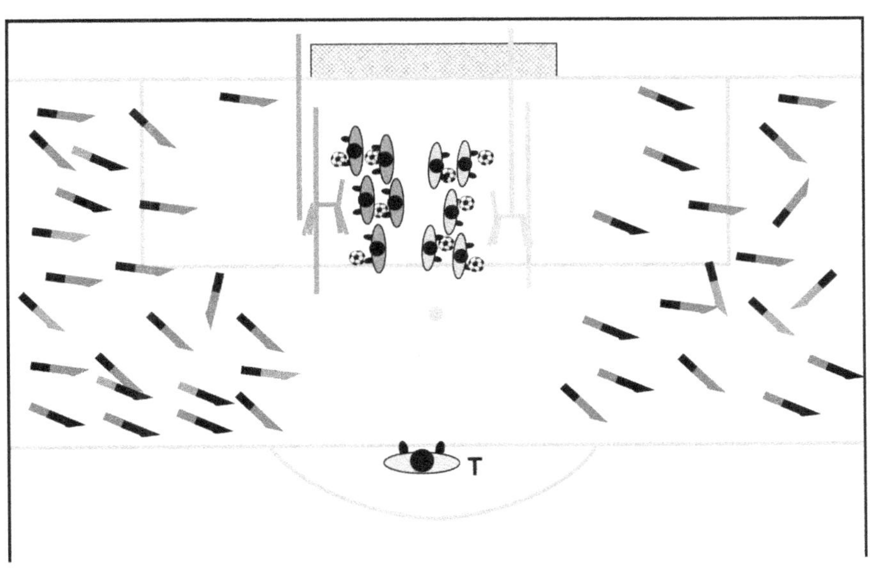

THE FLAGS

OBJECTIVES

Control of the ball.
Dribbling the ball in long strides.

EQUIPMENT

One ball per player.
Two flags and two cones.

AREA OF PLAY

An area suitable to the number of players involved.

PLAYERS

The players are divided into two teams.

ACTIVITY

The players on each team are lined up at a distance of 15 yards from a cone. The first player in each line has a flag in his hand. When the coach gives the signal, that player dribbles the ball in long strides as far as the cone opposite him, turns around the cone and dribbles the ball back. When he reaches the front of his line, he gives the flag to the teammate who is now first in line, and then goes to the back of the line. The teammate who has just received the flag dribbles the ball forward in long strides as far as the cone opposite him, turns around the cone and dribbles the ball back, giving the flag to the teammate who is now first in line, and so on. The game finishes when all the players have dribbled the ball around the cone, and one point is scored by the team that finishes first.

"THROW AND DRIBBLE"

OBJECTIVES

Development of the motor skills necessary to dribble the ball.
General coordination.

EQUIPMENT

One ball per player.

AREA OF PLAY

An area suitable to the exercise.

PLAYERS

The players are scattered on the field.

ACTIVITY

1. The players throw the ball upward and, after one bounce, dribble it for 5-6 yards.
2. The players throw the ball upward and, after spinning around, dribble it for 5-6 yards.
3. The players have the ball in their hands and their arms are stretched out; they drop the ball and kick it with the inside or the outside of the foot before it touches the ground, then they dribble it for 5-6 yards.
4. The players have the ball in one hand and their arms are spread out; they drop the ball and kick it with their foot before it touches the ground, then they dribble it for 5-6 yards. The exercise should be repeated several times, alternating the right and the left hand.
5. The players throw the ball upward behind their shoulders, then quickly turn around and try to intercept it with their foot before it touches the ground and dribble it for 5-6 yards.
6. The players have the ball on their right hand and their arms are spread out; they drop the ball and, before it touches the ground, they take a long sideways step to the right and then immediately dribble the ball with their left foot for 5-6 yards. They repeat the exercise with the ball on their left hand and taking a sideways step to the left to then dribble the ball with the right foot.
7. The players are opposite a wall, against which they throw the ball; after the bounce, they dribble the ball toward the direction called out by the coach.

"PULL THE TAIL AWAY" - THREE

OBJECTIVES

Control of the ball.
Speed of performance.
Individual work to dribble the ball.

EQUIPMENT

One ball per player.
Several cones.
A few pieces of plastic tape.

AREA OF PLAY

The penalty area.
Using the cones, one square per player is formed in the goal area portion of the penalty area, with an equal number of squares, equidistant from one another, arranged in each half of the goal area (see diagram).
In that portion of the penalty area which is outside the goal area, a few circuits are formed which will be used to dribble the ball.

ACTIVITY

One player, called player "A", positions himself at the center of the goal area (the players take turns acting as player "A"). The other players put a piece of plastic tape in their shorts, letting it hang out from the back of their shorts like a tail. Each player places himself inside one of the squares with the ball at his foot and, depending on the coach's direction, dribbles the ball forward, back, to the right, to the left. When the coach calls out "change", the players must dribble the ball into one of the squares which is in the other half of the goal area. But, as they move from their square to another, player "A" tries to pull the tail away from them. A player whose tail is pulled away is eliminated from the game and practices along one of the circuits in the penalty area. The winner is the player whose tail is not pulled away.

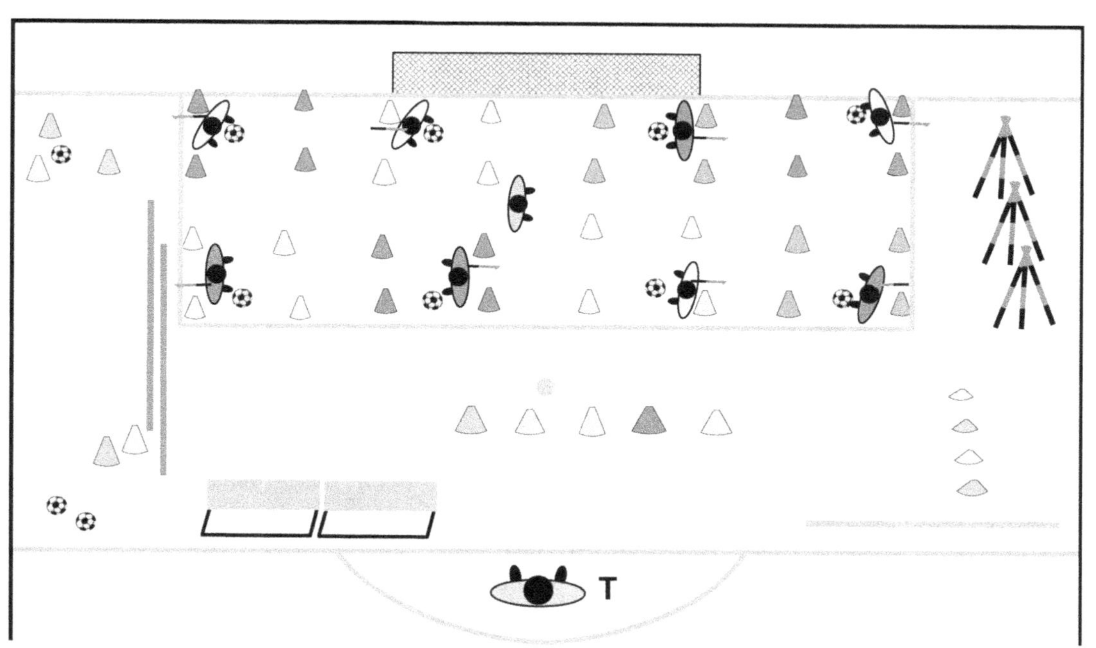

T

THE CHAIN

OBJECTIVES

Control of the ball.
Speed of performance.
Familiarizing with the group.

EQUIPMENT

One ball per player minus one.
A few pieces of plastic tape.

AREA OF PLAY

The penalty area.

ACTIVITY

One player, called player "A", positions himself on one side of the penalty area (the players take turns acting as player "A"). The other players, called players "B", each have a ball and a piece of plastic tape in their shorts, hanging out from the back of their shorts like a tail. Players "B" place themselves on the side of the penalty area opposite player "A". When the coach gives the signal, players "B" dribble the ball to the opposite side of the penalty area while player "A" chases them, trying to pull their tail away.

Players whose tails are pulled away join hands with player "A", forming a kind of chain. All together, without breaking the chain, they try to pull the tail away from the other players. The winner is the last player with a tail.

HERCULES

<table>
<tr><td>OBJECTIVES</td><td>Control of the ball.
Speed of performance.
Familiarizing with the group.</td></tr>
<tr><td>EQUIPMENT</td><td>One ball per player minus one.</td></tr>
<tr><td>AREA OF PLAY</td><td>The penalty area.</td></tr>
<tr><td>ACTIVITY</td><td>One player, called player "A", positions himself at the center of the penalty area without the ball (the players take turns acting as player "A"). His task is to be "Hercules": he must wrap his arms around a player who is dribbling the ball and lift him from the ground. The other players are arranged along each of the two short sides of the penalty area.
When the coach gives the signal, all the players dribble their balls from one side of the penalty area to the other. Player "A", "Hercules", chases them trying to wrap his arms around one of them and lift him from the ground. A player who is lifted from the ground also becomes a "Hercules" and, together with player "A", tries to catch the other players.
The game continues like this until there is one player left who has not become "Hercules": that player is the winner.</td></tr>
</table>

CLEARING THE FIELD - TWO

OBJECTIVES

Speed of performance.
Control of the ball.

EQUIPMENT

Several balls made of rolled up newspaper.
One regular ball per player.

AREA OF PLAY

Two concentric circles are formed by driving some poles into the ground. The size of the area of the smaller circle should be about the same size as the area of the ring formed between that smaller circle and the bigger circle. An equal number of balls formed with rolled up newspaper pages is scattered inside the smaller circle and inside the ring.

PLAYERS

The players are divided into two teams: teams A and B.

ACTIVITY

Team A is arranged inside the smaller circle while team B is arranged in the ring area created between the two circles. When the coach gives the signal, each player on each team picks up a "paper ball" while dribbling a regular soccer ball and throws the paper ball into the opponents' area. After a prescribed length of time, the coach stops the game; one point is scored by the team with the fewer "paper balls" in its area.

ADVICE

The players should be advised to throw the "paper balls" into those parts of the other team's area where, at that moment, there are no opponents.

"PULL THE TAIL AWAY" - FOUR

OBJECTIVES

Control of the ball.
Speed of performance.
Individual work.
Shooting at goal.

EQUIPMENT

One ball and one piece of plastic tape per player.
A few poles.

AREA OF PLAY

The penalty area.
A path is marked by using poles laid, end to end, on their side; the path is in front of the goal, about 2-3 yards from the goal area. It is 5-6 yards wide and 15 yards long. Circuits where players can dribble the ball are prepared outside the penalty area.

PLAYERS

Depending on their number, the players are divided into teams of 4 or 5 players each. The players on each team are numbered sequentially.

ACTIVITY

The players put a piece of plastic tape in their shorts, letting it hang out from the back of their shorts like a tail. They sit down forming a half-circle 4-5 yards from the path. The coach calls out a number and the players whose number corresponds to the number called immediately rise and start dribbling the ball along the path. As they dribble their ball along the path, they try to pull the tail away from the player who is in front of them, trying to avoid having theirs pulled away by the player behind. As soon as they get to the end of the path, they shoot at goal. The last player to shoot at goal is eliminated from the game, as is the player who is the first to have his tail pulled away. Then, these two players practice along the circuit formed outside the penalty area.
If, while dribbling, a player's ball goes outside the path, he must return to the beginning of the path and start over. The winner is the team with the fewest players eliminated at the end of the game.

TALKING ABOUT ONESELF - THREE

OBJECTIVES Listening.
Watching.

EQUIPMENT One ball per player.

AREA OF PLAY A suitable area.

PLAYERS They sit on the ground, forming a half-circle.

ACTIVITY

1. Sitting in front of the players, the coach introduces himself and tells something about himself. Every now and then, without taking his eyes off the players, the coach says "look at the eyes of the person who is speaking", trying to focus the attention of the players.

2. One at a time, the players take turns dribbling the ball. When the coach gives the signal, the player stops and starts telling something about himself while the others listen and look him in the eyes.

3. One at a time, the players take turns dribbling the ball while watching their teammates. While his teammates are telling something about themselves, the coach asks two of them to exchange places. When the coach gives the signal, the player who is dribbling the ball must stop and give the names of the teammates who have exchanged places.

4. One at a time, the players take turns dribbling the ball while watching their teammates, who are sitting. His teammates tell something about themselves, and while they are doing that, they pass a piece of plastic tape from one to another, hiding it in their closed fist. When the coach gives the signal, the player who is dribbling the ball must stop and give the name of the teammate who he thinks has the piece of plastic tape in his fist.

5. One at a time, the players take turns dribbling the ball while watching their teammates, who are sitting and telling something about themselves. The coach carries out a sequence of "claps"; for example, he claps his hands, he claps his hands on his knees, he claps his hands on his feet, etc.
When the coach gives the signal, the player who is dribbling the ball must stop and try to repeat at least three of the coach's claps.

6. One at a time, the players take turns dribbling the ball
   while watching their teammates who are telling something about themselves. The coach passes the ball with
   his hands to some of them. When the coach gives the
   signal, the player who is dribbling the ball must stop
   and give the names of the teammates to whom the
   coach has passed the ball with his hands.

FASTER THAN THE BALLOON

OBJECTIVES

Quickness of reflex.
Developing techniques.

EQUIPMENT

One ball per player.
A few chairs, a few pieces of plastic tape and a balloon.

AREA OF PLAY

The midfield circle.
Two parallel lines of chairs are arranged inside the mid-field circle about 5-6 yards apart.
The distance between the chairs is about 7-8 yards; on each chair there is a piece of plastic tape.

PLAYERS

The players are divided into two teams: teams A and B.
The players on each team are numbered sequentially.

ACTIVITY

The players on each team are sitting and are lined up in numerical order. Each team is positioned in front of a line of chairs. The coach has the balloon in his hand and stands at the end of the two lines of chairs. He calls out a number and throws the balloon upward. Each team's player whose number corresponds to the called out number gets up and, as quickly as possible, dribbles his ball to the first chair in his team's line of chairs, where he stops the ball and picks up the piece of plastic tape from the chair. Then, with a long touch, he dribbles the ball to the second chair, where he stops the ball and picks up the piece of plastic tape from that chair, and so on, going from chair to chair, until the balloon touches the ground. When the balloon touches the ground, the coach calls out "stop". The players stop and the one who has more pieces of plastic tape scores a point for his team.
The players should carry out several repetitions of this exercise.

ADVICE

1. The players with the same number on each team should have comparable skills.
2. The players should be asked to dribble the ball from one chair to another with only one long touch so that they can run faster.
3. The players should stop the ball near the chairs using the inside of the foot.

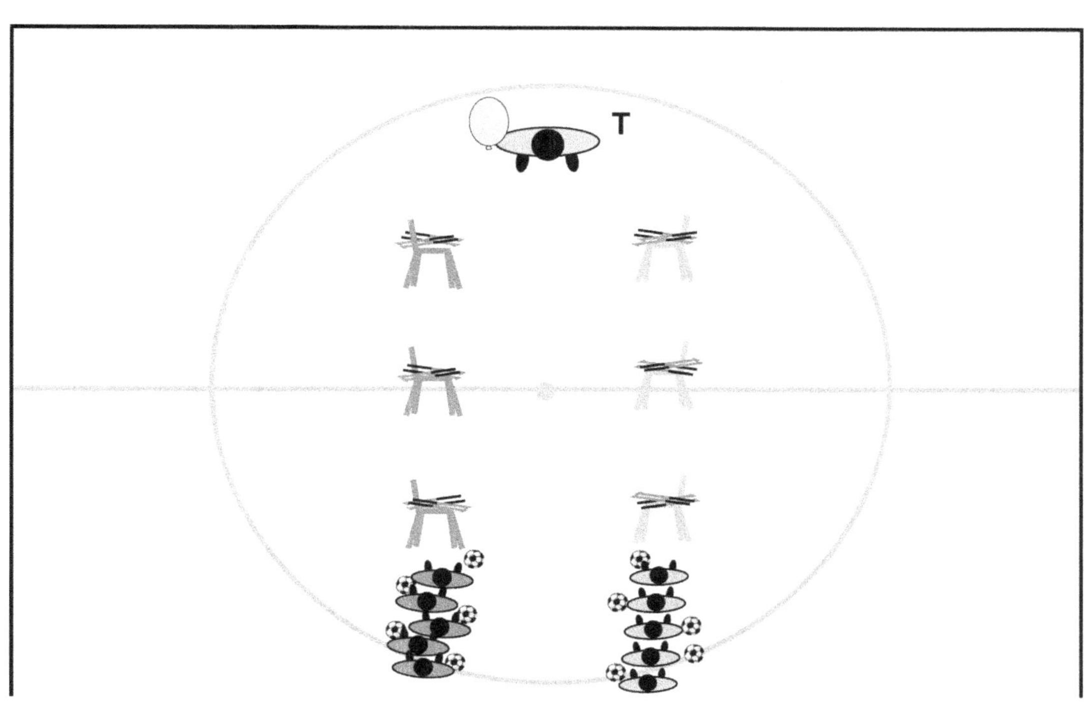
T

"DRIBBLE AND SHOOT AT GOAL"

OBJECTIVES

Speed of performance.
Dribbling the ball.
Shooting at goal.

EQUIPMENT

Several balls and empty plastic bottles.
Eight mats.

AREA OF PLAY

The penalty area.
The penalty area is divided into two parts by a line of cones which is perpendicular to the area's long side (see diagram). Many plastic bottles are scattered randomly in the penalty area, leaving very few empty spaces. 4 mats are placed in each of the halves of the penalty area, in empty spaces among the bottles. Next to each mat there is a ball.
Along the goal line, a small goal is placed in each half of the penalty area.

PLAYERS

The players are divided into two teams.
The players on each team are numbered sequentially.

ACTIVITY

Each team is assigned one of the two halves of the penalty area. The players of each team are sitting, arranged in numerical order, just outside their assigned area. When the coach calls out a number, the two players whose number corresponds to the called out number get up and each dribbles his ball toward a mat. When they reach the mat, they shoot at the small goal and immediately dribble the ball that is next to the mat toward another mat in their area; when they reach it, they take another shot at goal and immediately dribble the ball next to that mat, and so on from one mat to another, all the time trying to avoid knocking down the plastic bottles.
Meanwhile, one player per team takes turns retrieving the balls shot at goal and putting them back next to the mats for the next player.
A player finishes his exercise after having shot all the balls next to the mats.
A player scores one point each for his team:
- for being the first to shoot all the balls at goal;
- for finishing his circuit while knocking down the fewest bottles:
- for having sent the highest number of balls into the goal.

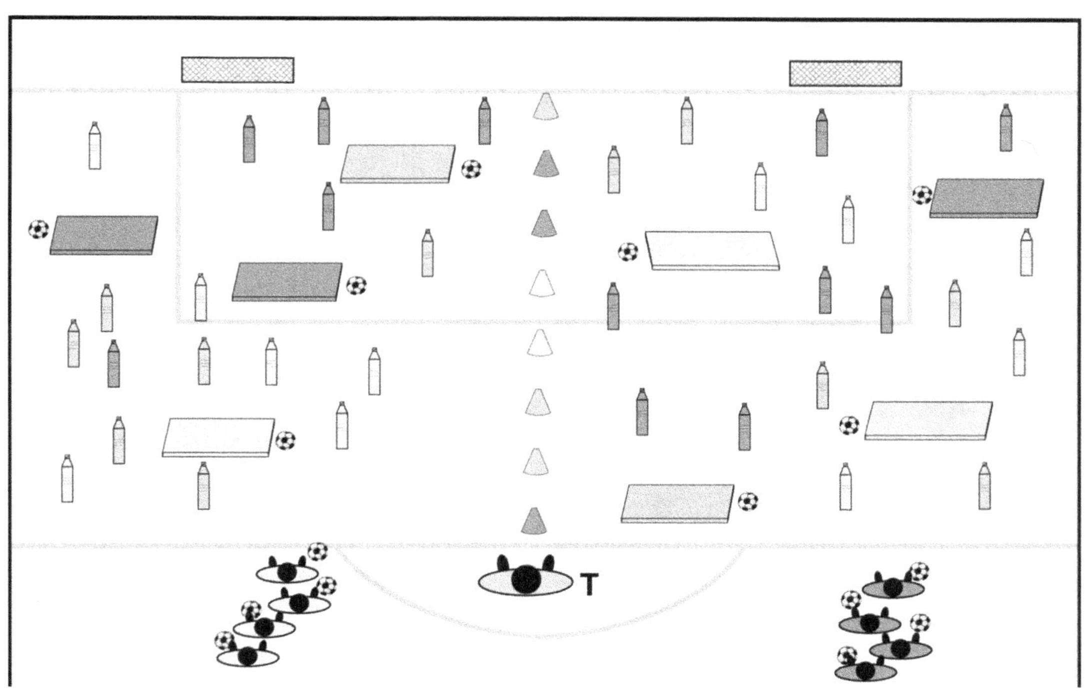

T

ON THE SAME WAVE-LENGTH - ONE

OBJECTIVES

Control of the ball.
Respecting one's teammate's skills.
Waiting one's turn.

EQUIPMENT

One ball per player.

AREA OF PLAY

The penalty area.

PLAYERS

The players are divided into two teams.
The players on each team are numbered sequentially.

ACTIVITY

The players of each team are lined up and are sitting just outside one of the shorter sides of the penalty area.
Two players, one from team A ("A1") and the other from team B ("B1") are arranged on the opposite side of the penalty area, each across from his own team.
When the coach gives the signal, "A1" and "B1" dribble the ball toward their own team and, once they reach their team, join hands with their teammate number 2 ("A2" and "B2", respectively). "A2" and "B2" get up and, holding hands with their teammate (A1 and B1), go back to the starting point with each player dribbling his ball. Once they get to the starting point, "A1" and "B1" sit down just outside the penalty area, while "A2" and "B2" repeat the action of "A1" and "B1". The exercise goes on like this until the two teams are lined up on the side opposite to the one where they were at the beginning. One point is scored by the team that is first to finish.

"DRIBBLE AND SCORE"

OBJECTIVES

Speed of performance.
Touching the ball purposefully.
Shooting at goal.

EQUIPMENT

One ball per player.
A few poles.

AREA OF PLAY

Just outside the goal area and in front of the goal, a few poles are laid on their side to mark two circuits consisting of alternating segments, as follows: a curve to the right, a curve to the left, a straight segment. The length of each segment is not fixed.

PLAYERS

The players are divided into two teams, A and B.
The players on each team are numbered sequentially.

ACTIVITY

Each team is assigned a circuit. The players of each team are arranged in a row, with their backs to the circuit. Each time the coach calls out a number, the two players whose number corresponds to the number called out get up and start dribbling their ball down their assigned circuit. At the end of the circuit, they shoot at goal. In the goal there is a goalkeeper who is not a member of either team. If the ball goes outside the circuit, the player must go back and start again. The player who is the first to finish the circuit scores a point and he can score an additional point if he scores a goal. The exercise continues until each player on each team has dribbled the ball down the circuit a prescribed number of times.

ADVICE

1. The players with the same number should have comparable skills.
2. The players should be asked to dribble the ball at one touch for each segment of the circuit so that they can run faster.

"LET'S GO ROUND THE FIELD"

OBJECTIVES

Speed of performance.
Feinting.

EQUIPMENT

One ball per player.
A few poles and cones.

AREA OF PLAY

A few poles are laid on their side to outline a rectangle. The four corners of the rectangle are marked by using the cones.

PLAYERS

The players are divided into four teams: A, B, C and D. The players on each team are numbered sequentially.

ACTIVITY

Each team is assigned one corner of the rectangle and practices a different feint. When the coach gives the signal, players "1" on each team dribble the ball round the field and return to their starting point. The players on team A and B dribble the ball around the field counter clockwise, while the players on team C and D dribble the ball around the field clockwise. When they get back to their starting point, players "1" restart practicing the feint, while players "2" immediately start and do the same exercises that players "1" have just done. The exercise goes on like this until the last player has dribbled the ball around the field. Four points are scored by the team that finishes first, three by the team that finishes second, two by the team that finishes third and one by the team that finishes last.

**EXERCISES TO BE
CARRIED OUT ON THE
CORNERS OF THE FIELD**

- Dribbling the ball forward, in a straight direction; every 3-4 touches, the players should stop the ball with the sole of their foot and then immediately start dribbling again.
- A line of small posts is arranged on the ground. The players should dribble the ball forward, parallel to the line of small posts. Each time they are along the same line as a small post, they should feint stopping the ball with the sole of the foot, and instead kick it forward using a long touch.
- A line of small posts is arranged on the ground about 4-5 yards apart. The players should dribble the ball

from one small post to the next using straight touches; when they are close to a small post, they should feint shooting, and instead dribble the ball by weaving through the small posts.

- A line of small posts is arranged on the ground. The players should dribble the ball from one small post to the next using straight touches. When they get close to a small post, they should carry out a "double step". This is carried out as follows: If they are dribbling the ball with the right leg, they pass the right leg over the ball, and then dribble the ball forward using the inside of the left foot. Vice-versa if they are dribbling the ball using the left leg. A variation is that the players should step over the ball with the right leg, and then dribble the ball forward to the left using the inside of the right foot or using the outside of the left foot.

IN THE CIRCLES

OBJECTIVES

Speed of performance.
Developing skills.

EQUIPMENT

One ball per player.
A few poles and cones.

AREA OF PLAY

Each team is assigned a square that is marked on the ground. At each corner of each square, a few poles are placed to outline a circle. A line of 4-5 cones is placed in the middle of each side of each square. The distance between the cones is about 1-1.5 yards.

PLAYERS

The players are divided into two teams, A and B, and on each team the players are numbered sequentially.

ACTIVITY

The players of each team are arranged in a row outside their assigned square. Each time the coach calls out a number, the players whose number corresponds to the number called dribble their ball into the first circle to their left if they dribble the ball counterclockwise (on the other hand, if they dribble the ball clockwise, they dribble their ball into the first circle to their right); then they go on and dribble the ball through the cones, enter the second circle and, turning left - if they dribble the ball counterclockwise (on their right if they dribble the ball clockwise) - they go on this way till they get back to the initial circle. The team that is the first to reach the initial circle scores a point. The exercise continues until each player has dribbled the ball round the area of play a prescribed number of times.

ADVICE

1. The players with the same number should have comparable skills.
2. In order to develop speed, the players should be required to dribble the ball through the cones, and then from the cones to the circles, at one touch each.

PASS COMPETITION

OBJECTIVES

Speed of performance.
Cooperating even while competing with each other.

EQUIPMENT

Two balls for each group.
A few poles.

AREA OF PLAY

One square per team is outlined on the ground. At each corner of each square, a few poles are placed to outline a circle. Each circle is given a sequential number.

PLAYERS

The players are divided into groups of 6 players each.

ACTIVITY

Each group places one player in each of the circles on the corners of their square. A fifth player, called player "A", has a ball and is placed outside the square; his task is to pass the ball to his teammates in each of the circles. The sixth player, called player "B", has a ball too, and is placed in one of the circles, prepared to dribble the ball. When the coach gives the signal, player "A" passes the ball to his teammate inside circle 1, who passes it back to him. Then, player "A" passes it to his teammate inside circle 2, who passes it back to him, and so on until the ball is passed again to the player in circle 1.

At the same time, player "B" dribbles out of his circle and goes around the square until he returns to the circle from which he started. "B" scores a point if he gets to the end of his circuit before "A" has passed the ball to, and received the ball from, each of the four players in the four circles. The game finishes when all the players of the group have played the role of "player B" a prescribed number of times. The winner is the player who has scored more points.

CONTEST - ONE

OBJECTIVES

1 on 1.
Tackling.
Waiting one's turn.

EQUIPMENT

One ball.
Four cones.

AREA OF PLAY

The cones are used to mark a 10x10-yard square.

PLAYERS

The players are divided into two teams: teams A and B.
In each team, the players are numbered sequentially.

ACTIVITY

The coach is outside the square with the ball in his hands. Facing each other, the two teams are arranged in rows, in numerical order, at a distance of 7-8 yards from the square.
Suddenly, the coach throws the ball into the square and calls out a number. The players with the called out number immediately rush to the square to take possession of the ball and start a "1 on 1". Using his feet, the player who manages to get with the ball beyond any side of the square scores a point for his team. The game continues like this until each player has played the 1 on 1 a prescribed number of times.

ADVICE

The skills of the players with the same number on each team should be comparable.

MAD ROPE - TWO

OBJECTIVES

Improving space skills.
Improving timing.
Dribbling the ball.

EQUIPMENT

One ball per player.
A few cones and a rope.

AREA OF PLAY

The penalty area.
The cones are placed in the penalty area to outline one square per player.

PLAYERS

The players are divided into two teams.

ACTIVITY

Each player takes his respective square and carries out ball dribbling exercises.
Meanwhile, the coach moves across the penalty area while swinging the rope in a circle, horizontal to the ground, sometimes slowly and sometimes very fast. While they practice ball dribbling, the players must pay attention so that they are not hit by the rope. Each time a player is touched by the rope, he must knock down one cone in his square. At the end of the prescribed time, one point is scored by the team with more cones still standing.

BALL DRIBBLING EXERCISES

- The players dribble the ball in a straight direction; then they dribble it to the right using the inside of their left foot, or using the outside of their right foot; then they dribble it to the left using the inside of their right foot, or using the outside of their left foot.
- The players touch the ball with the inside of their right foot and immediately afterwards use the inside of their left foot, so as to bring the ball back toward the point where they touched it first.
- The players slightly touch the ball with the inside of their right foot and immediately use the outside of their left foot, so as to make it roll toward the direction given by the first touch. Then they slightly touch it with the inside of their left foot and immediately use the outside of their right foot.

"MOVE ON THE CHAIRS"

OBJECTIVES

Balance.
Dribbling the ball.

EQUIPMENT

Three chairs and a ball per team.
A few poles.

AREA OF PLAY

The goal area.
Two areas, called "K" and "K1", are outlined on one short side of the goal area by three or four posts lying on their side. Each team is given one of these two areas to practice dribbling the ball.

PLAYERS

The players are divided into two teams, teams A and B.

ACTIVITY

Each team is lined up outside the line opposite zones "K" and "K1". One player per team, player "A1" and player "B1", are placed inside their respective zones. When the coach gives the signal, they start practicing an exercise prescribed by the coach.

The first in each line can reach his zone to practice the exercises only by "walking" on three chairs. He gets on one chair and moves forward by turning around, picking up a chair, and placing it ahead of the chair on which he is standing. He sets them down, one after the other, and walks on them, rotating his upper body to retrieve the chair that is left behind him and places it in front of the other two. Once he gets to his zone, he practices dribbling while his teammate ("A1" or "B1") goes back to his team "walking" on the three chairs. When he reaches his team, another teammate starts and the game goes on until the last player's turn. One point is scored by the team that finishes the game first.

BALL DRIBBLING EXERCISES

- The players feint a shot and dribble the ball sideways with the inside of the foot.
- The players run with the ball, slow down and fake stopping, then start running again with a spurt (this is a useful move in a match, when the opponent is running close by).
- The players dribble the ball straight-ahead, step over the ball while moving their body to the side they feinted, and immediately touch the ball toward the opposite side, using the outside of the same foot.

100

"PULL THE TAIL AWAY" - FIVE

OBJECTIVES

Improving relationships; there are no winners or losers.
Quickness of reflex.
Improving skills with group exercises.

EQUIPMENT

One ball per player.
Pieces of plastic tape and cones.
A few pieces of equipment to form circuits.

AREA OF PLAY

The midfield circle.
A few cones are placed to form "save" bases inside the
midfield circle, near the circumference.
As many circuits to dribble the ball are formed as the
number of players. The circuits are formed at different
distances from one another.
The circuits should be different from one another, be
proportionate to the players' skills and the players should
be familiar with them.

PLAYERS

The players are divided into equal groups, depending on
their number.
Each player is numbered sequentially (in the above
example, from 1 to 7).
Then, the grouping criterion is changed: the groups are
formed with the players who have the same number (all
players "1", and so on).
All the players, except those of a group called "A", have a
piece of plastic tape in their shorts which hangs out like a
tail.

ACTIVITY

Each group practices dribbling the ball along one circuit.
The coach moves around the area of play and suddenly
gives the signal by raising his arms. The players with the
"tails" immediately run to the "save" bases, chased by the
players of group "A", who try to pull their tail away
before they get to the bases. The game restarts with the
groups that resume dribbling the ball along a circuit. Also,
the players whose tails have been pulled practice dribbling
the ball with their teammates. However, when the coach
gives the next signal, they act as "chasers".
Every now and then, the coach puts two groups together,
or he makes two groups exchange circuits, so that all the
players can meet each other and all the groups can
practice all the circuits.
The game finishes when all the players have lost their tail.

BALL GATHERING

OBJECTIVES

Speed of performance.
Control of the ball.

EQUIPMENT

Several balls.

AREA OF PLAY

A rectangular space the size of which depends on the
number of players. (it should not be too large)
Near the sides of the area of play, three small "gathering
spaces" are outlined. The players must gather the balls in
them.

PLAYERS

The players are divided into three teams, A, B and C.

ACTIVITY

An equal number of balls is placed inside each "gathering
space". Other balls are scattered here and there on the
area of play. Each team is assigned one of the three
"gathering spaces", and an opponent is placed in each
space. The opponent's task is to kick the balls (which are
in the "gathering space") out of it into the area of play,
continuously and one after the other, while the other
players dribble the ball toward their respective "gathering" space.
When the prescribed time is over, the balls inside each
team's "gathering" space are counted. The team with the
highest number of balls in its "gathering" space scores a
point.

ADVICE

1. The players on all three teams should have comparable
   skills.
2. The "opponents" who are in the "gathering" spaces
   and who kick the balls out of them should be required
   to kick the balls toward their own teammates.

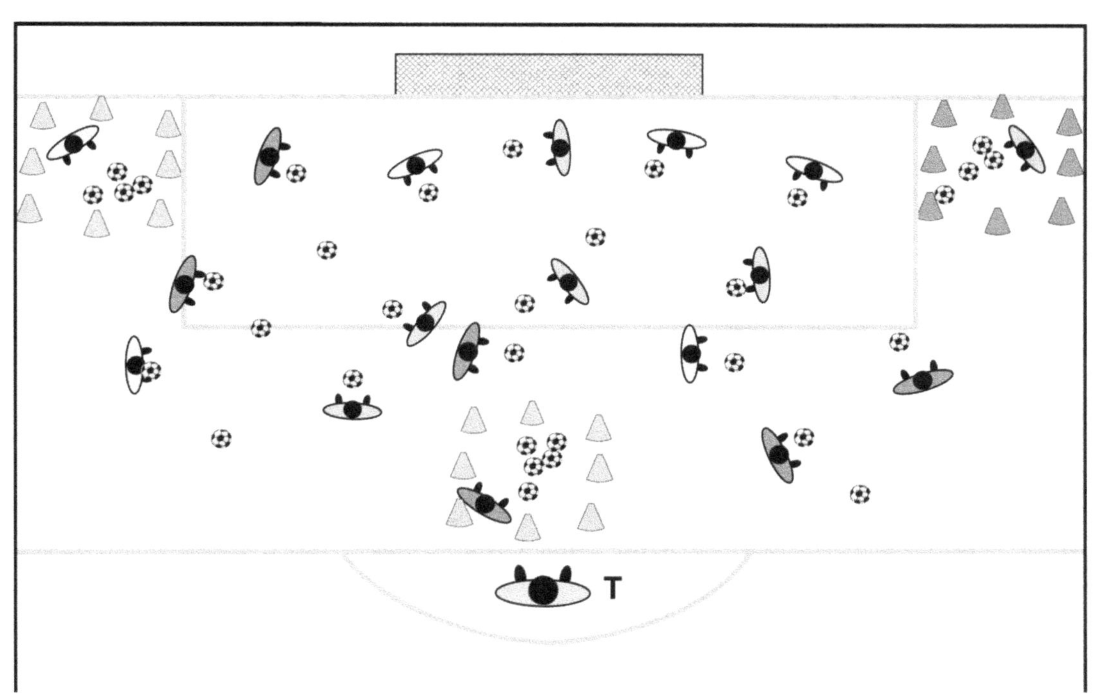

T

"COME FIRST" - ONE

OBJECTIVES

Speed of performance.
Control of the ball.
Looking ahead.

EQUIPMENT

One ball per player.
A few pieces of plastic tape.
A few cones.

AREA OF PLAY

The goal area, in which a few cones are scattered.

PLAYERS

The players are divided into two teams, A and B.

ACTIVITY

The teams are arranged in single file, opposite each other on the end lines of the area of play.
When the coach gives the signal, all the players start dribbling the ball at pace toward the opposite side. The player who is last to reach the other end line puts a piece of plastic tape into his shorts, letting it hang out like a tail.
In the next repetitions, this player starts as first in his line. More repetitions are carried out, in a number corresponding to the number of players. At the end, the "tails" are counted; the winner is the team with fewer "tails".

ADVICE

1. The skills of the players on the two teams should be comparable.

A PASS TO BE SAFE

OBJECTIVES

Cooperating even while competing with each other.
Visualizing.

EQUIPMENT

One ball per player, minus two.

AREA OF PLAY

The penalty area, or any other space suitable to the number of players, around which a few workstations are placed to practice certain skills.

PLAYERS

The players are scattered in the area of play, each with a ball except two: player "A" and player "B".

ACTIVITY

Player A is placed at edge of the area of play and acts as a "chaser". Player B is placed with the other players for whom he acts as a "helper"; when the exercise starts, he will have to watch them, keeping an eye on the ball of the teammate who is chased. When the coach gives the signal, the game starts and all the players dribble their ball in the area of play, paying attention to player A who, within a prescribed amount of time, tries to tag them with his hand.

When player A touches a player, the latter is eliminated and gets out of the area of play and practices some exercises at a workstation while the exercise continues. However, if a player who is being chased manages to pass the ball to the "helper" (player B) before being touched, then he is not eliminated and does not leave the field. In this case, player B starts dribbling the ball and the player who passed him his ball becomes the new "Player B".

After a prescribed length of time (3-5 minutes), a new repetition is started with a different player acting as a "chaser".

The game finishes when all the players have acted as "chasers". The winner is the player who manages to eliminate the highest number of players.

VARIATIONS

1. With large numbers, then there can be two "helpers", or the players can be divided into 5 to 6-player groups, with each group having its own "helper". Of course, in this case the ball can only be passed to the "helper" in one's own group.
2. The "chaser" wears a hat as a distinctive mark, and when he touches a player they switch roles. The player who has been touched becomes the chaser; he takes the hat from the other player and gives him the ball. The player who now has the ball can move 10-15 yards away from the present chaser before being chased.

CONTESTING

OBJECTIVES

1 on 1.
Waiting one's turn.
Forcing the opponent toward a disadvantaged direction.

EQUIPMENT

One ball, four poles and eight cones.

AREA OF PLAY

The poles are driven into the ground to form a 10x10-yard square.
In the middle of each side two cones are placed to form a small goal, C, D, E and F, on each side of the square.

PLAYERS

The players are divided into two teams, teams A and B. Each player in each team is sequentially numbered.

ACTIVITY

The coach is outside the area of play. The two teams are arranged opposite each other and the players are sitting in a row in numerical order 4-5 yards from the area of play. The coach calls out a number and kicks the ball into the center of the square. The players with the called out number run into the square to take possession of the ball and start a 1 on 1. Player A attacks small goals C and D and defends small goals E and F. Player B attacks small goals E and F and defends small goals C and D. When either of them dribbles the ball beyond the goal line of one of the small goals he is attacking, he scores a point for his team. The game continues like this until all the players have been involved in the 1 on 1 for a prescribed number of times.

ADVICE

There should not be too much difference in the skills of the players with the same number.

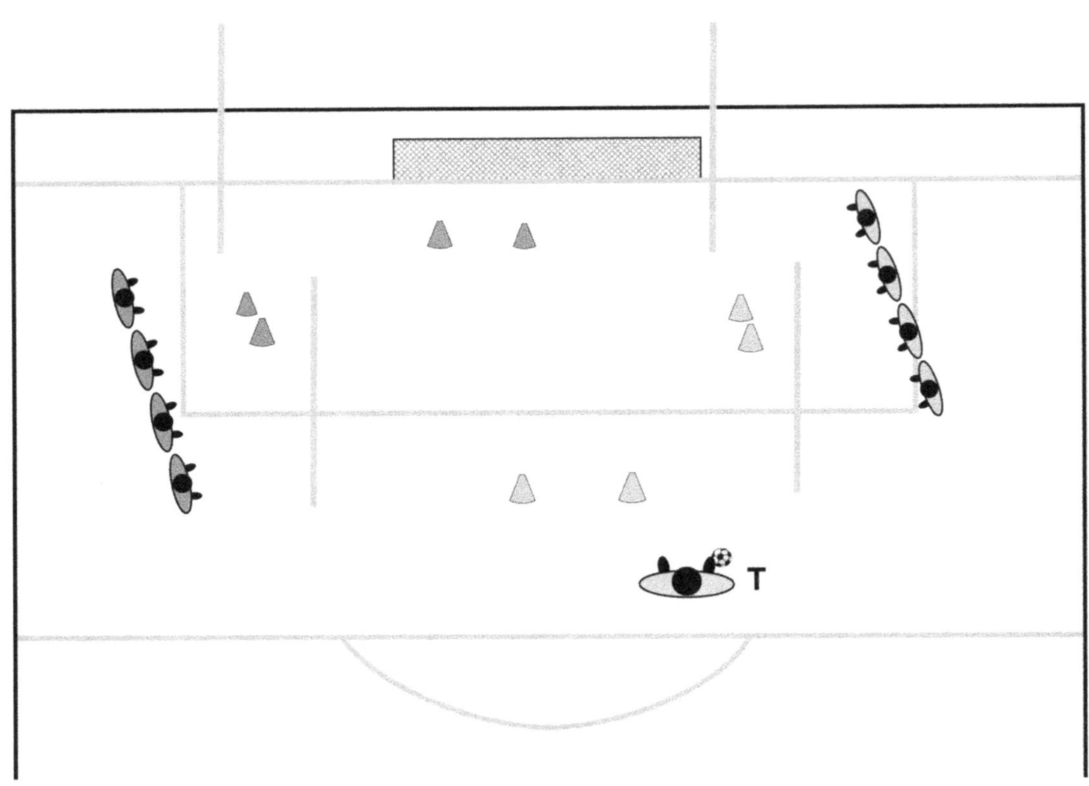

"DEFEND FROM A SITTING POSITION"

OBJECTIVES

Practice control of the ball.
Waiting one's turn.

EQUIPMENT

One ball for every player acting as attacker.
A few cones.

AREA OF PLAY

The cones are used to form a number of squares corresponding to the number of players in team B. The squares are arranged in a row 2-3 yards apart.

PLAYERS

The players are divided into two teams, team A and team B. Team A attacks, team B defends.

ACTIVITY

Team A is arranged at a distance of 5-6 yards from the row of squares. Each player in team A is given a sequential number. Team B places one player in each square; this player sits on the ground with his legs bent and his hands on the ground. When the coach gives the signal, team A's player number 1 ("A1") starts dribbling the ball toward the first square. When A1 enters the square, defender "B" raises his pelvis from the ground and moves trying to tackle him. If defender B manages to touch the ball with his feet, he scores a point for his team. On the other hand, whenever player A1 goes beyond a square without his ball being touched he scores a point for his team. A1 does this with each of the squares. Each player of team A and team B practices these roles. When each player on team A and each player on team B have had turns playing these roles, their roles as "attacker" and "defender" are exchanged, and, at the end of the exercise, the winner is the team with the highest score.

TO THE SQUARES

OBJECTIVES

Speed of performance.
Lateralization.
Quickness of reflex.

EQUIPMENT

Cones and balls.

AREA OF PLAY

The penalty area, where the cones are used to form a few small squares here and there.

PLAYERS

The players are divided into two teams whose players are numbered sequentially.

ACTIVITY

Team A's players are arranged in a row on the end line of the area of play, and each of them has two balls. Team B's players are in a seated position and are scattered inside the area of play.

When the coach calls out a number, team A's player with the called number, using only one hand, throws one of the two balls as far as possible. Immediately afterwards, he starts dribbling the other ball trying to reach one of the squares which has been created in the area of play. Meanwhile, the player in team B who has that called out number must quickly retrieve the ball thrown by his opponent and dribble it toward the area of play. When player B enters the goal area portion of the penalty area with the ball at his feet, the coach calls out "stop" and player A must stop. Team A scores a point for every square that player A has reached before the "stop". More repetitions should be carried out and the roles of the players should also be exchanged.

ADVICE

1. The players with the same number should have comparable skills levels.
2. The players should alternate the arm used to throw the ball.

"REMEMBER"

OBJECTIVES

Visual perception and memory.
Feinting.

EQUIPMENT

One ball per player.
Cones and poles.
Various objects (no more than 20), for example tennis balls, table tennis balls, paper rolled into a ball, different kinds of corks, cards of different colors.

AREA OF PLAY

Two rectangles, placed close together, one for each team; the long sides of the rectangles are marked with poles at a distance of 3-4 yards from one another, while the short sides are marked with cones at a distance of 2-3 yards from one another.

PLAYERS

The players are divided into two teams.

ACTIVITY

The coach puts the various objects into the two rectangles. The players study the objects for 20-30 seconds. Then the objects are covered with something, for example a shirt. When the coach gives the signal, the players of the two teams start dribbling their ball, weaving along the sides of the rectangle; when they reach the first pole, they carry out a feint before weaving through the next poles. Meanwhile, the coach uncovers the objects and picks up one object that he hides in the shirt he is holding in his hands. The players are asked to study the remaining objects and state which object the coach has removed. A player scores a point for his team when, while dribbling the ball, he guesses within 20 seconds which object the coach has removed. After 20-30 seconds, the coach covers the objects again, and the exercise is repeated.

EXAMPLES OF FEINTS

- The players move to the right, step over the ball, and immediately dribble the ball with the outside of their left foot.
- The players feint a pass to the left and instead continue to dribble the ball.
- The players move the ball to the left with the inside of their right foot, and then quickly move the ball to the right by touching it with the outside of their right foot.
- The players dribble the ball forward with their left foot, step over the ball with their left leg, and quickly dribble

the ball forward using the inside of their right foot.

- The players dribble the ball forward with their left foot, step over the ball with their left leg, and, when the ball is close to their left foot, move the ball to the right with the inside of their left foot.
- The players dribble the ball forward, touch it first with the inside of their right foot, and then quickly touch it with the inside of their left foot, so that the ball goes back toward the point where it was touched first.

ADVICE

At the beginning, a small number and very distinguishable objects should be used; then, the number of objects should be increased, and the objects used should be less distinguishable.

MUSICALLY - TWO

OBJECTIVES

Overcoming shyness.
Increasing speed of performance.

EQUIPMENT

One ball and a long piece of plastic tape per each player of team B; the tape should be hanging out from the back of the shorts of players B like a tail and should touch the ground.

AREA OF PLAY

A circle formed by the two teams; the players are sitting in numerical order, one behind the other, with the side of their head toward the center of the circle.

PLAYERS

The players are numbered sequentially and are divided into two teams: team A (the chasers) and team B (the chased).

ACTIVITY

When the coach gives the signal, both teams start singing a song, with each player drumming with his hands on the back of the player who is sitting in front of him. When the coach calls out a number; the player of team B having that number must dribble the ball around the circle and get back to the starting point while being chased by the player of team A with the same number, who tries to pull the "tail" away from player B by stepping on it before B gets back to the starting point. The drill finishes when each player has been called a pre-established number of times; then the roles are exchanged.
The chasing team scores a point for every tail it pulls away, while the chased team scores a point every time its player gets back to the starting point with his "tail".

ADVICE

The skills of the players having the same number should be comparable.

PASSING FROM HAND TO HAND

OBJECTIVE

Increasing speed of performance.

EQUIPMENT

Team A has only one ball, while the players of team B have a ball each; a few posts and cones.

AREA OF PLAY

A circle formed team A players, who are sitting in numerical order.

A lane ("K") is formed by laying some poles on their side, and in this lane there are a few randomly placed cones.

PLAYERS

The players are divided into two teams, team A and team B, and are numbered sequentially.

ACTIVITY

The coach is in the center of the circle formed by team A. Team B is lined up in numerical order in front of lane K. When the coach gives the signal, player A1 passes the ball from hand to hand to the player next to him, and that player to the next player and so on, and the coach counts the number of times the ball returns to player A1. At the same time, team B starts dribbling the ball through lane K with player B1 starting the drill; as soon as he gets to the end of the lane, player B2 does the same thing, then player B3 and so on. When all the players of team B have dribbled the ball through the lane, the coach stops the exercise and writes down how many times the ball returned to player A1. Then, the roles are exchanged.

One point is scored by the team that manages to pass the ball completely along the circle the greatest number of times.

Several repetitions should be carried out.

VARIATION

Team B is lined up outside a circle formed by team A players.

While the team A players pass the ball around their circle, from hand to hand, team B players take turns dribbling the ball around the circle.

TUNNEL - ONE

OBJECTIVES	Dribbling the ball with zig-zagging movements. Touching the ball purposefully. Guided control. Waiting one's turn.
EQUIPMENT	One ball and two hurdles per team. A few cones and other hurdles.
AREA OF PLAY	An area suitable to the number of players.
PLAYERS	The players are divided into three teams and are numbered sequentially.
ACTIVITY	Each team is lined up in numerical order.

In front of the first player of each line, at a distance of 2-3 yards, 5 or 6 cones are lined up 2-3 yards apart. Beginning at a distance of 3 yards from the last cone, two or three hurdles are lined up. When the coach gives the signal, the first player in each line (player 1) starts dribbling the ball, weaving through the cones, touches the ball with the inside of the foot to pass it under the hurdles; then he quickly runs to the right or to the left of the line of hurdles and, with the inside of the foot, controls the ball which is passing out from under the last hurdle. He turns back and passes the ball to teammate 2, and then sits down at a distance of 5-6 yards from the hurdles. Player 2 carries out a guided control of the ball with the inside of the foot, does the same exercise as player 1 and at the end passes the ball to teammate 3 and sits down behind teammate 1.
The game continues like this until each player has had his turn.
One point is scored by the team that finishes first.

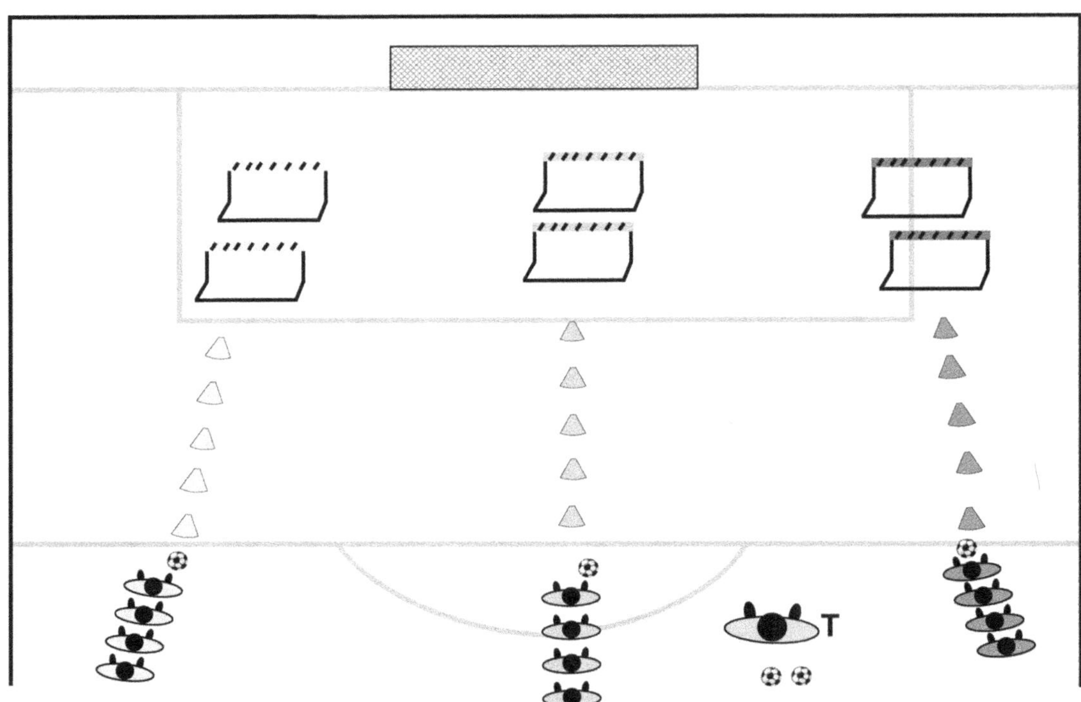

T

"THE FORBIDDEN ZONE"

OBJECTIVES

Speed of performance.
Control of the ball.

EQUIPMENT

One ball per player, plus one ball for the coach.
A few cones and posts.

AREA OF PLAY

The goal area, or any rectangular space suitable to the number of players.
A few posts are placed diagonally beginning at the corners of the rectangle, creating four triangular zones: C, D , E and F.
A few cones are scattered here and there in zones C and D; zones E and F are zones where the players are forbidden to stop.

PLAYERS

The players are divided into two teams, A and B.

ACTIVITY

Each team is arranged in a row along each short side of the rectangular area of play, while the coach stands on one of the long sides. When the coach gives the signal, he kicks his ball high up. Each player on each of the two teams quickly starts dribbling his ball straight to the opposite side of the area of play, without touching the cones and without stopping in the forbidden zones. When the ball kicked by the coach touches the ground, the coach calls out "stop" and all the players must stop where they are. One point is scored by the team with fewer players in zones E and F, and one point is scored by the team with more players close to the target (the side opposite to where they have started from).

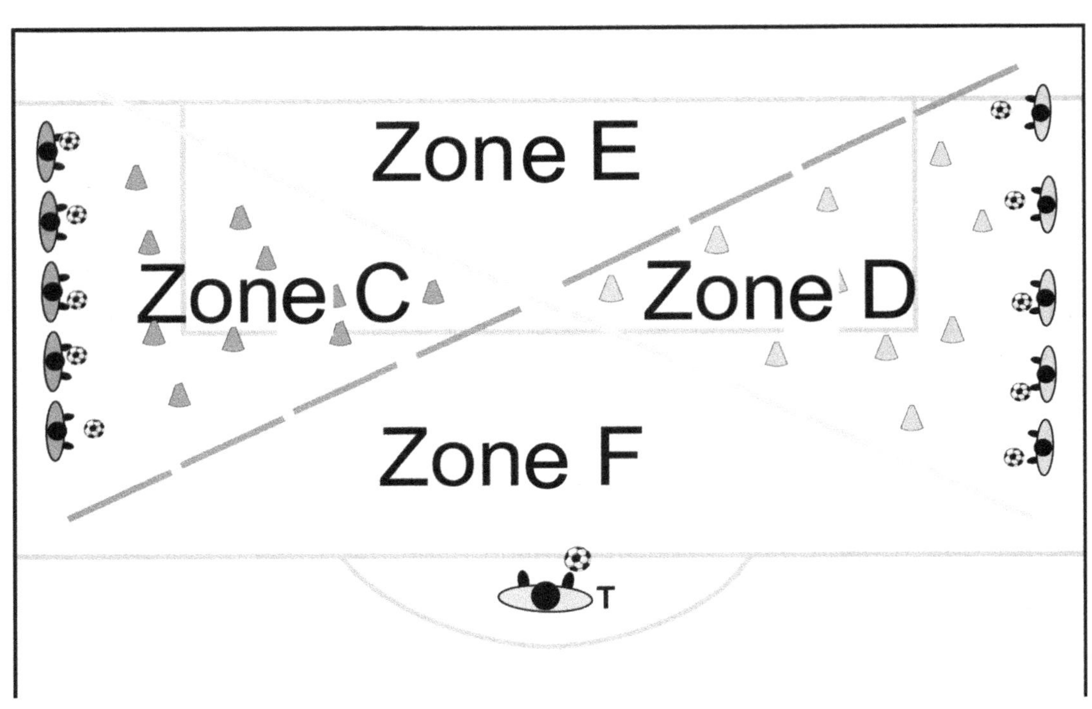

Zone E
Zone C
Zone D
Zone F
T

TARGET PRACTICE

OBJECTIVES

Dribbling the ball and shooting.
Visualizing.
Feinting.

EQUIPMENT

One ball only.
Two cones per player.
A few pieces of plastic tape.

AREA OF PLAY

A space suitable to the number of players.

PLAYERS

The players are arranged in a circle 2-3 yards apart with their legs wide apart.

ACTIVITY

Each player has two cones behind him. One player, player "A", is inside the circle with the ball at his feet, and dribbles it in the direction given by the coach. When the coach gives the signal, player "A" must immediately, or after a feint, shoot the ball through a teammates' legs, trying to hit the small cones which are behind the teammate. The player whose cones are targeted must try to intercept the shot with the inside of the foot.
Player "A" repeats the exercise three times. The players whose small cones are hit must put a piece of plastic tape hanging out from the back of their shorts like a tail.
The players take turns acting as player "A", and the exercise continues until each player has acted as "A" a pre-established number of times. The winner is the player with fewer "tails" at the end of the exercise.

ADVICE

In order to be successful in hitting the small cones, the player in the center should be advised to note which teammates are not paying attention and to immediately, or after a feint, shoot the ball through their legs.

THE NEWSPAPER OF SAFETY

OBJECTIVES

Control of the ball.
Quick coordination.

EQUIPMENT

One folded newspaper and one ball per player.

AREA OF PLAY

The goal area, or any space suitable to the number of players.

ACTIVITY

One player, player "A", acts as a "chaser". The other players each have a ball at their feet and are holding a newspaper. When the coach gives the signal, player "A" starts chasing the other players while dribbling his ball, trying to touch another player. The other players are dribbling their balls too, and must avoid being touched. When they are about to be touched, they should drop the newspaper that they are holding and jump onto it with their feet close together. If a player is touched before he can jump onto the newspaper, he becomes a chaser and exchanges roles with player "A". To avoid players moving about too little for fear of being touched, the coach should set a total maximum length of time for which a player is allowed to use his newspaper as a "safety device" (for example, 5 or 6 seconds).

This exercise can be made more interesting by dividing the field into two halves: when the coach gives the signal, the players must try to reach the opposite side and the player who comes in last does not participate in the next repetition.

"CRAWL UNDERNEATH"

OBJECTIVES

Body coordination.
Control of the ball.
Waiting one's turn.
Spine mobility.

EQUIPMENT

One ball per team.

AREA OF PLAY

A space suitable to the number of players.

PLAYERS

The players are divided into two teams.

ACTIVITY

The two teams are lined up, at a distance of about 4-5 yards from one another. The players are standing with their legs wide apart. When the coach gives the signal, the first player of each line turns toward his teammates who are behind him and crawls on all fours under his teammates' legs while pushing the ball forward with his chest over the ball. When he reaches the end of the line, he stands up and dribbles the ball back to the next player in line, and then runs to the back of the line. The player who has received the ball does the same exercise, which continues in the same way until all the players have carried it out.
One point is scored by the team whose players are the first to finish the exercise.

VARIATION

In each line, the players are alternately standing with legs wide apart or with legs close together. The player who is doing the exercise crawls on all fours under the players whose legs are wide apart, and crawls on all fours around those players whose legs are close together.

ON THE SAME WAVE-LENGTH - TWO

OBJECTIVES

Control of the ball.
Adjusting to one's teammate's skills.

EQUIPMENT

Two poles per each pair of players.
Three balls per player.

AREA OF PLAY

The penalty area.

PLAYERS

The players are divided into pairs.

ACTIVITY

The players of each pair are placed one behind the other and they each have a ball at their feet. They are standing along one short side of the area of play. In each pair, the players are holding between them the end of a pole in each hand, forming a kind of stretcher with the poles: the two poles are parallel to each other and are at the height of the players' pelvis, and the coach places a ball between the two poles. When the coach gives the signal, the pairs dribble their balls toward the opposite side of the area of play, without letting the ball on the poles fall. If that ball falls, the pair goes back to the beginning and starts again. A point is scored by the pair that is first to reach the opposite side.

ADVICE

The pairs should be formed by a better and a less skillful player (the better player should be in the front).

ON THE SAME WAVE-LENGTH - THREE

OBJECTIVES

Control of the ball.
Adjusting to one's teammate's skills.

EQUIPMENT

One ball per player.
A few poles.

AREA OF PLAY

The penalty area.

PLAYERS

The players are divided into groups of 5 players each.

ACTIVITY

The players in each group form two parallel lines of two players each, with the fifth player placed between the two lines. The two players in each line hold a pole on both of their shoulders. The fifth player is placed between the two lines inside the space marked by the two poles on one side and the two poles on the other side. Each group is placed on one of the short sides of the area of play in a row with the other groups. Each player has a ball. When the coach gives the signal, the groups move forward while dribbling the ball in a coordinated way; the fifth player in each group must be careful to remain in the space formed by the four poles, otherwise his group will have to return to the beginning and start again. One point is scored by the group that is the first to get to the opposite side.

ADVICE

The groups should be formed by players of mixed ability.

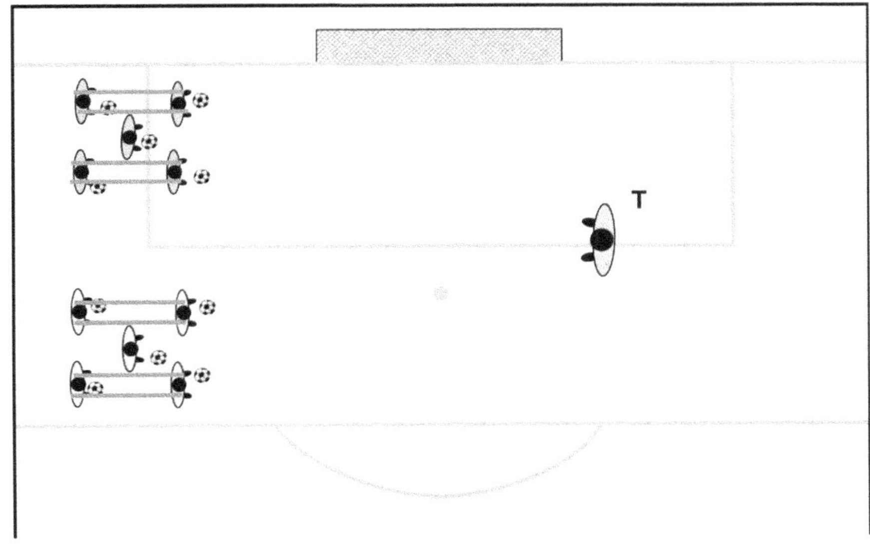

OBJECTIVES

Guided control.
Quickness of reflex.

EQUIPMENT

Small poles and cones.
One ball.

AREA OF PLAY

The penalty area.
The cones are used to form a rectangle, which is a size suitable to the number of the players.
This rectangle is divided into two halves by a broad row of small poles, which act as a "net".
Using four cones, two squares ("K" and "K1") are formed in the middle of each of the two halves.

PLAYERS

The players are divided into two teams (team "A" and team "B") consisting of 9 players each.

ACTIVITY

The two teams are each arranged in one of the two halves of the area of play, like in volleyball. One player per team is placed inside the square in the middle; for example, player "A9" is placed in square "K" and player "B9" is placed in square "K1". Their task is to serve the ball by kicking it to the opposite side. The coach decides which of the two teams should start serving, for example team "A". Then, player "A9" serves the ball by kicking it over the net toward the opposite side. One opponent carries out a guided control of the ball before it touches the ground, dribbles it toward teammate "B9" and gets back to his own position. Player "B9", inside square "K1", kicks the ball back to team "A"'s side and so on.
A team scores a point whenever the opposing team's kick falls out of the area of play. A point is also scored when ever an opponent controls the ball after it has touched the ground.
As in volleyball, the players rotate when there is a change of possession.

ADVICE

This exercise is particularly suitable for a gymnasium.

RESPECT YOUR TEAMMATE'S SKILLS

OBJECTIVES

Control of the ball.
Adjusting to one's teammate's skills.

EQUIPMENT

Various items of equipment: small poles, long rods, cones, balls.

AREA OF PLAY

Various spaces, suitable to the number of the players.

PLAYERS

The players are divided in different ways: into 3-player groups, into two teams, into pairs.

ACTIVITY

1. The players are divided into groups of 3 players each. A few items of equipment are used to prepare a circuit in which to dribble the ball (see diagram). Each group holds a small pole at hip's height or over the head, and carries it while dribbling the ball along the circuit.
2. The players are divided into two teams. Each team holds a long rod and all the players of each team carry it from one end of the goal area to the other. The team that comes in first scores a point. Several repetitions should be carried out.
3. The players are divided into pairs and are placed in a square formed by four cones. In each pair, the players are standing back to back, holding the ball between the lower part of their backs, pushing against each other with equal force. Keeping this position, they move about inside the square while dribbling a ball in a coordinated way.
4. The players are divided into pairs. A line of cones 2-3 yards apart is prepared for each pair. While holding his teammate's hand, one player dribbles the ball through the cones while his teammate dribbles it sideways along the cones. Or, both players, standing one behind the other and holding each other's hand (the player in the front holds with his right hand the left hand of his teammate behind him), dribble the ball through the cones.

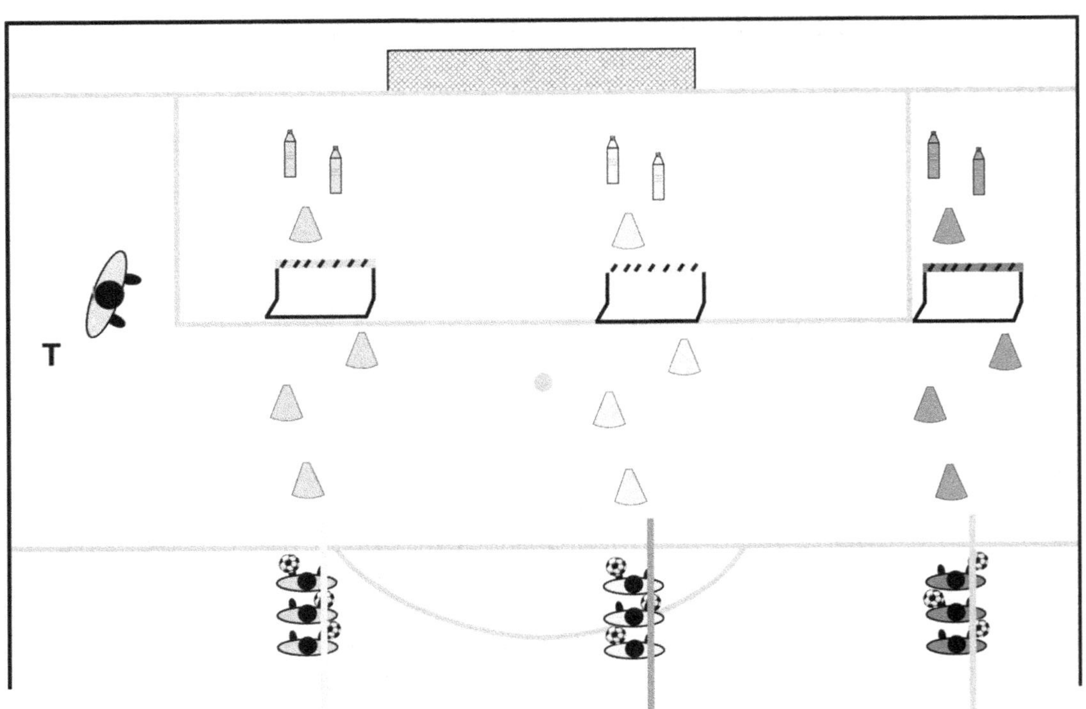

T

DRIBBLING RELAY

OBJECTIVES

Increasing speed of performance.
Dribbling the ball with zigzagging movements.

EQUIPMENT

Cones, balls and poles.

AREA OF PLAY

A space suitable to the number of the players.

PLAYERS

The players are divided into two teams, and on each team the players are numbered sequentially.

ACTIVITY

The players of each team are arranged in two rows which are facing each other, 15 yards separating the two rows, with the players with even numbers being arranged sequentially in one row and those with odd numbers arranged sequentially in the other row. The two teams should be placed rather far from one another.

A line of cones is formed from player number 1 (in one row) to player number 2 (his opposite player in the other row). Then, a line of cones is formed from player number 2 to player number 3, then from number 3 to number 4 and so on as far as the last teammate. When the coach gives the signal, player 1 in each team starts dribbling the ball with weaving movements through the line of cones toward teammate 2, taking him the ball. When he receives the ball, player 2 starts dribbling the ball with weaving movements through the line of cones between him and teammate 3, taking him the ball. In turn, player 3 carries out the same exercise, taking the ball to teammate 4, and so on. The exercise continues until the last player dribbles the ball through a "goal" formed by two poles in the middle of the area of play (see diagram).

One point is scored by the team that comes in first through the goal.

After each repetition, the players should exchange their numbers in order to take different positions and so that each player can act once as the one who dribbles the ball through the goal.

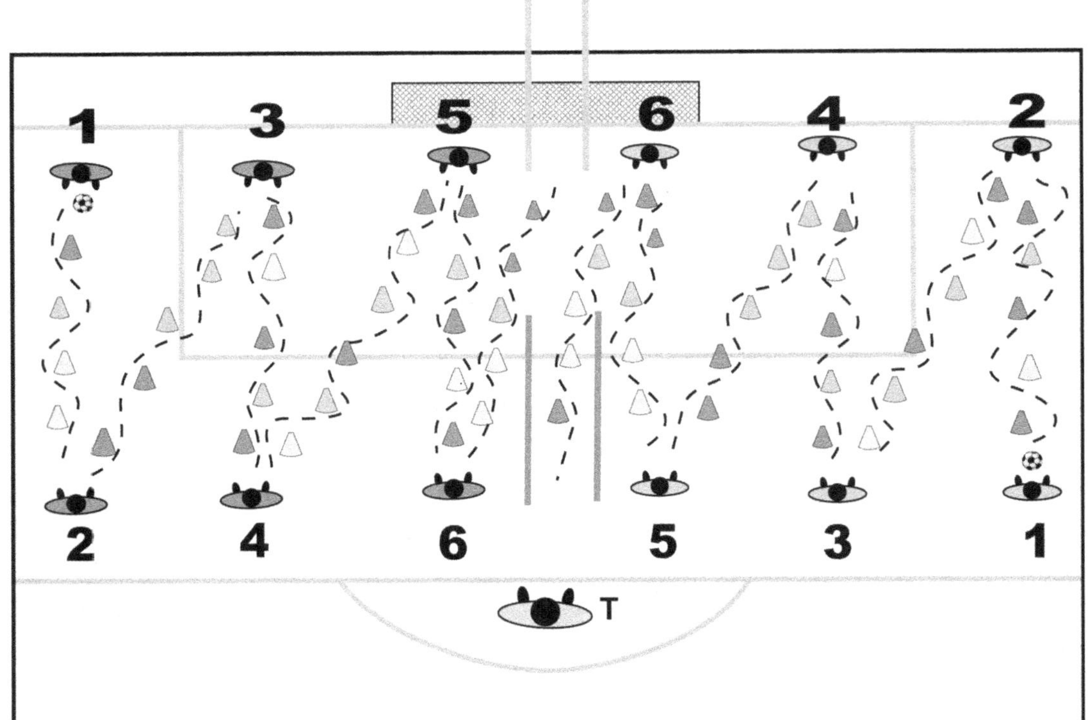

1
3
5
6
4
2
2
4
6
5
3
1
T

"COME FIRST" - TWO

OBJECTIVE	Speed of performance.
EQUIPMENT	One ball per player.
AREA OF PLAY	A suitable space.
PLAYERS	The players are divided into two teams ("A" and "B"), and on each team the players are numbered sequentially.
ACTIVITY	All the players of team "A" (except one, player "A1") are arranged in a circle together with players "B", holding hands. "A1" dribbles the ball around the circle formed by the other players. The coach calls out a number. "A1" starts dribbling the ball faster, while the player of team B corresponding to that number starts quickly dribbling his ball around the circle in the direction opposite to "A1"'s direction.

A point is scored by the player who is the first to reach the place vacated by the player of team B whose number has been called. The player who comes second continues dribbling the ball around the circle; then, the coach calls out another number for the next repetition and the same exercise is done.

The game finishes when each player has carried out a pre-established number of repetitions.

IMPORTANT — The player whose number is called must dribble the ball in the direction opposite to the direction of the other player so that the two of them meet at a certain point. To prevent them from bumping into each other, the coach should ask the player whose number he has called to dribble the ball close to the circle, while the other player should dribble it while keeping himself a bit further away from the circle. Also, the players should be asked to look ahead every now and then while dribbling the ball.

"HE WHO SCORES GETS OUT"

OBJECTIVES

Dribbling the ball with zigzagging movements and passing.
Accepting different roles.

EQUIPMENT

A few cones.
One ball.

AREA OF PLAY

A small sized field with two goals.
Four lines, consisting of 5-6 cones each, are placed along the sidelines and outside the area of play. The distance between the cones should be about 2 yards.

PLAYERS

The players are divided into 5-player teams, without the goalkeepers.

ACTIVITY

Two opposing teams are placed on the field, each positioned in one half of the field. Each team is designated one of the two sidelines with its related lines of cones. When the coach gives the signal, the teams play a game without the goalkeepers. During the game, the player who scores a goal must get off the field and place himself by the line of cones outside the sideline that has been designated to his team. He is not allowed to get back into the field, but whenever the ball goes over the sideline that was assigned to his team, he must get the ball, dribble it with zigzagging movements weaving through "his team's" line of cones and then pass it to one of his teammates who is still on the field. When more than one player is off the field, the player who carries out the dribbling is the one who is closer to the ball when it leaves the field.
The winner is the team to get all its players off the field.

VARIATION

When he is about to make the pass, the player who is outside the field calls the name of the teammate to whom he wants to pass, and who will try to break away from marking.
For the action to be successful, the coach will ask the player who makes the pass to call a teammate who is free from marking when the pass is about to be made.

"LOOK FOR YOUR TEAMMATE" - ONE

OBJECTIVES

Watching.
Increasing speed of performance.

EQUIPMENT

One ball per player.
A few cones.

AREA OF PLAY

A space suitable to the number of the players.
Using cones, a few rectangular spaces are outlined behind the area where the players dribble the ball.

PLAYERS

The players are scattered in the dribbling area.

ACTIVITY

The players are scattered in front of the coach. Three or four players have a piece of plastic tape tied around their head, and they are positioned away from the others. Each of the players dribbles his ball in the direction shown by the coach. When the coach gives a pre-established visual signal, each player dribbles his ball into one of the rectangles outside the dribbling area, forming groups of two or three players in each rectangle. However, in each rectangle there can be only one player who has plastic tape around his head, and therefore each rectangle must be occupied by one player with plastic tape around his head and no more than two other players (of those without plastic tape on their heads). The players who do not fit in a group do not participate in the next repetition.

"LOOK FOR YOUR TEAMMATE" - TWO

OBJECTIVES

Watching.
Dummy movement.

EQUIPMENT

One ball.

AREA OF PLAY

A space suitable to the number of the players.

PLAYERS

All the players are arranged in a circle, except one (player "A") who is placed in the center of the circle.

ACTIVITY

The players are arranged in a circle around player "A" who has the ball. The coach gives the signal and calls out the name of a player; player "A" dribbles the ball to that player, who moves towards him. When they are close to each other, player "A" passes him the ball and, with a dummy movement, goes to the place vacated by his teammate. Meanwhile, the player who now has the ball dribbles it toward another player whose name has been called out by the coach and passes him the ball. The game continues like this until each player has carried out a pre-established number of repetitions.

ADVICE

The player with the ball should call out the name of the next player to be involved before the player who has passed the ball carries out the dummy movement; in this way, the players practice both watching the ball and peripheral vision.

"ME!"

OBJECTIVES	Controlling the ball. Cooperating even while competing with each other.
EQUIPMENT	One ball per player.
AREA OF PLAY	The penalty area.
PLAYERS	The players are scattered in the area of play and dribble the ball without restrictions.
ACTIVITY	Before starting the game, two players are chosen, perhaps player "A" and player "B". Player "A" has to chase player "B". When the coach gives the signal, all the players start dribbling their balls around the area of play. Player "A" runs after player "B" trying to catch him while both of them are dribbling their balls. However, if another teammate touches player "A" on the shoulder shouting "me!", player "A" must give up chasing player "B" and start chasing that player. The same applies the next time another player touches him on the shoulder shouting "me!". When player "A" manages to touch the player after whom he is running, that player becomes the next "chaser".
ADVICE	If player "A" has run enough without managing to catch another player, the coach should relieve him to exchange roles.

"DON'T GET BUMPED INTO"

OBJECTIVES

Eye-hand coordination.
Control of the ball.
Speed of performance.
Quickness of reflex.

EQUIPMENT

A few car tires.
One ball per player.

AREA OF PLAY

The goal area.

PLAYERS

The players are divided into three or four teams.

ACTIVITY

All the teams except one (team "A") are arranged along one of the short sides of the goal area. The players of team "A" are arranged opposite the others, along the other short side. Each player on team "A" has one tire. When the coach gives the signal, the players on team "A" push their tires to try to disturb the action of the other players, who are dribbling their balls across the goal area, trying to reach the opposite side. One point is scored by the team whose players all reach the opposite side first. The game finishes when all the teams, in turn, have pushed the tires across the area of play a pre-established number of times.

VARIATION

One rope is tied around each tire. The team that has the task of disturbing the others is permitted to use only the rope to move the tires from one side of the area of play to the other.

134

"DON'T GET ANGRY"

OBJECTIVES

Tackling with the shoulders.
Showing emotion.
Containing impulse.

EQUIPMENT

One ball for each pair of players.

AREA OF PLAY

A space suitable to the number of the players.

PLAYERS

The players are divided into pairs.

ACTIVITY

If the total number of players is not even, one player takes acts as a referee. If the players are even, the coach is the referee. When the coach gives the signal, one player in each pair ("player A") dribbles the ball in the direction shown by the coach, while the other player ("player B") stays in body contact with player A, using his body to push him away from the ball.

When the coach gives a pre-established signal, player B, using his elbows too, pushes player A "too hard", and player A simulates a fall. At this point all B players simulate a moment of anger: they ignore player A and turn to the referee, raising their forefinger. Then they stand on one leg with the other leg bent back, keeping their arms outstretched with the palms of their hands turned upward, and keeping their heads bowed with their eyes looking down to the ground. Meanwhile, the A players make the following movements slowly and one after the other: first, they lower their socks, then they pull them up, finally they take a long breath. These actions are intended to make time go by in order to help the players overcome their anger and re-establish a certain emotional balance before acting instead of acting on impulse. After a pre-established number of repetitions the players exchange their roles.

ADVICE

While dribbling the ball, the players should keep their arms slightly bent and close to their sides to avoid the improper use of arms and elbows.

"COME FIRST" - THREE

OBJECTIVES

Increasing speed of performance.
Dribbling the ball around the circle using zigzagging movements.

EQUIPMENT

One ball per player.

AREA OF PLAY

A suitable space.

PLAYERS

The players are divided into three teams; on each team, the players are numbered sequentially.

ACTIVITY

All the players are sitting in a circle, with their legs crossed and a ball in their laps.
The coach is in the center of the circle and calls out a number. The players whose number corresponds to the one called start dribbling their balls in the same direction, zigzagging between their sitting teammates. The player who comes back first to his place scores three points; two points are scored by the player who comes in second and one point is scored by the player who comes in third. The game continues until each player has dribbled the ball around the circle for a pre-established number of times.

ADVICE

The skills of the players having the same number should be comparable.

"CHECK YOUR POSTURE"

OBJECTIVES	Checking one's own posture. Acquiring and developing skills.
EQUIPMENT	One ball per player. Chairs, benches, pieces of plastic tape or ropes. Walls with several faces, with each face about 50 inches wide and 45 inches high.
AREA OF PLAY	The penalty area. The walls should be arranged in such a way as to form an equilateral triangle with a 10-12 yard side; rows of chairs and benches should be placed near the walls. For each player, two poles are placed at a distance of 6-7 yards from each other, and a piece of plastic tape or a rope is tied between the two poles.
PLAYERS	The players are scattered on the field.
ACTIVITY	The players dribble their balls toward the walls, then kick the ball against one of them, and, after the ball bounces back, dribble it toward another wall; they kick the ball against the other wall, then dribble it toward another wall and so on.

When the coach calls out "to the poles!", the players dribble their balls toward the poles and, once they get there, using the outside or the inside of the foot, they softly kick the ball beyond the plastic tape. Then, on all fours, they pass under the piece of plastic tape, stand up, and, with a soft touch, kick the ball back under the piece of plastic tape, and go back on all fours and follow the ball until they reach it, and so on. Once the exercise is over, they go back to the walls and kick the ball against them again.

When the coach calls out "to the chairs!", the players dribble their balls toward the rows of chairs, pick up their balls with their hands, stretch their arms upward and walk on tiptoe on one row of chairs. Then they go back to kicking the balls against the walls.

When the coach calls out "recover!", the players commence breathing exercises.

When the coach calls out "to the benches!", the players dribble their balls to the benches and pick up their balls with their hands. They kneel down on one side of the bench; then with outstretched arms roll the ball forward

on the bench, keeping their chest low, till they reach the
end of the bench, and dribble the ball back toward the
walls.

When the coach calls out "to the walls!", the players carry
out a pre-established exercise by the walls ten times, then
they restart dribbling their balls.

**EXERCISES BY
THE WALLS**

- The players are sitting with legs crossed in front of the
wall, arms stretched upward and outward, with their
hands against the wall; they push their chest toward the
wall while stretching their arms upward, holding their
head tight between their arms.

- The players kneel down, sitting on their heels, in front
of the wall with their arms and palms of their hands
on the wall: they slowly push their chest downward.

- The players are sitting with legs crossed, with their
back against the wall and with their arms inside their
thighs; they push against the thighs with their arms
stretched and, while keeping the back of their head
against the wall, they move the chin back (as if taking
an uppercut to the chin).

- The players are sitting with their back against the wall;
they bend the upper body forward while keeping their
arms up. Then, with arms up and chins back, they raise
their upper body slowly until it fully contacts the wall.

ADVICE

The ball should be slightly touched with the outside of
the right foot (or of the left foot), then it should
immediately be touched again with the inside of the right
foot; then it should be touched with the outside of the
other foot to cause it to continue in the direction given by
the inside of the right foot, then it should be deflected to
the right with the inside of the left foot.

"COME FIRST" - FOUR

OBJECTIVES

Increasing speed of performance.
Dribbling the ball around a circle.

EQUIPMENT

One ball per player.

AREA OF PLAY

A space suitable to the number of players.

PLAYERS

The players are divided into two teams, and on each team the players are numbered sequentially.

ACTIVITY

The players of each team are sitting on the ground, with each team forming a circle. The two circles must be along the same imaginary line 5-6 yards from each other. The coach calls out a number and the player of each team whose number corresponds to the called out number quickly gets up and starts dribbling his ball around the circle formed by his teammates. One point is scored by the player who is first to return to his own place.

ADVICE

The skills of the players with the same number on each team should be comparable.

VARIATION

The player whose number is called dribbles the ball by weaving through his teammates.

2 ON 1 STRENGTH GAME

OBJECTIVES	Strength training. Cooperating even while competing with each other. Increasing speed of performance in a contest.
EQUIPMENT	One ball per player. A few poles.
AREA OF PLAY	The penalty area. Inside the penalty area, a rectangle (called "K") is outlined by laying down a few poles at a distance of 4 yards from each side of the penalty area.
PLAYERS	The players are divided into pairs, and all the pairs are divided into two groups: M and N.
ACTIVITY	The pairs of players take turns performing the exercise as follows. One pair in group M consists of players we will call players "B" and "B1" and one pair in group N consists of players we will call players "A" and "A1". The exercise involves one player from the group M pair and both players from the group N pair. The three players (B, A and A1) sit in the semicircular space just outside the penalty area, while all the other players sit inside the goal. When the coach gives the signal, all the players of groups M and N (except B, B1, A and A1) get up and start dribbling their balls along the perimeter of rectangle K, with each group dribbling the ball in opposite directions to return to their starting point. While all of the other group M and group N players are dribbling around the perimeter of the rectangle, B, A and A1 do the following exercise: without their balls, pair "A-A1" tries to catch player "B", who tries to escape. They can seize him by the arm or leg, and must try to drag him into the goal area. Player "B" must try to break free from them. The pair scores a point if they manage to drag player B into the goal area before all the other players of groups M and N have finished their perimeter-dribbling exercise and returned to their starting point. After each repetition, the pair and the player are relieved and replaced by three others. After a pre-established number of repetitions, the winner is the pair with the highest score.

"FOLLOW THE ORDERS"

OBJECTIVES

"Seeing" things and the ball.
Improving ability to vary the touch of the ball.
Improving teamwork.

EQUIPMENT

Small goals and poles.
Small items of equipment and series of objects of any kind.
For each group, a number of balls equal to the total number of players in that group, minus one.

AREA OF PLAY

For each team, a 12-15 yard long and 3-4 yard wide lane is outlined by laying the poles on the ground. Small pieces of equipment and various objects are scattered inside the lanes.
A small goal is placed at one end of each lane.

PLAYERS

The players are divided into groups of 4-5 players each.

ACTIVITY

One player ("A") from each group places himself in the small goal which is at one end of his group's lane; all the other players in that group (collectively, "B") line up at the opposite end. The first player in each line starts dribbling the ball through the lane while following player A's instructions, for example: "dribble the ball as far as the right hand side of the chair", "dribble the ball as far as the red bag", "dribble the ball behind the white bag", "put your right hand on a cone", etc. When the dribbling player reaches the end of the lane, he shoots at goal and takes the place of player A; the latter dribbles the ball back and goes to the back of his team's line. The player at the front of the line then repeats the dribbling exercise. This sequence is repeated until the time pre-established for end of the exercise.

ADVICE

1. Practice using one foot at a time.
2. The player who is dribbling the ball must reach the object specified by teammate A by touching the ball only once.
3. Player A must give the next order a few moments before the player with the ball gets to the object specified in the prior order - this will make the action move faster and smoother.
4. The groups should be comprised of players with a full range of ability (from poor to excellent).

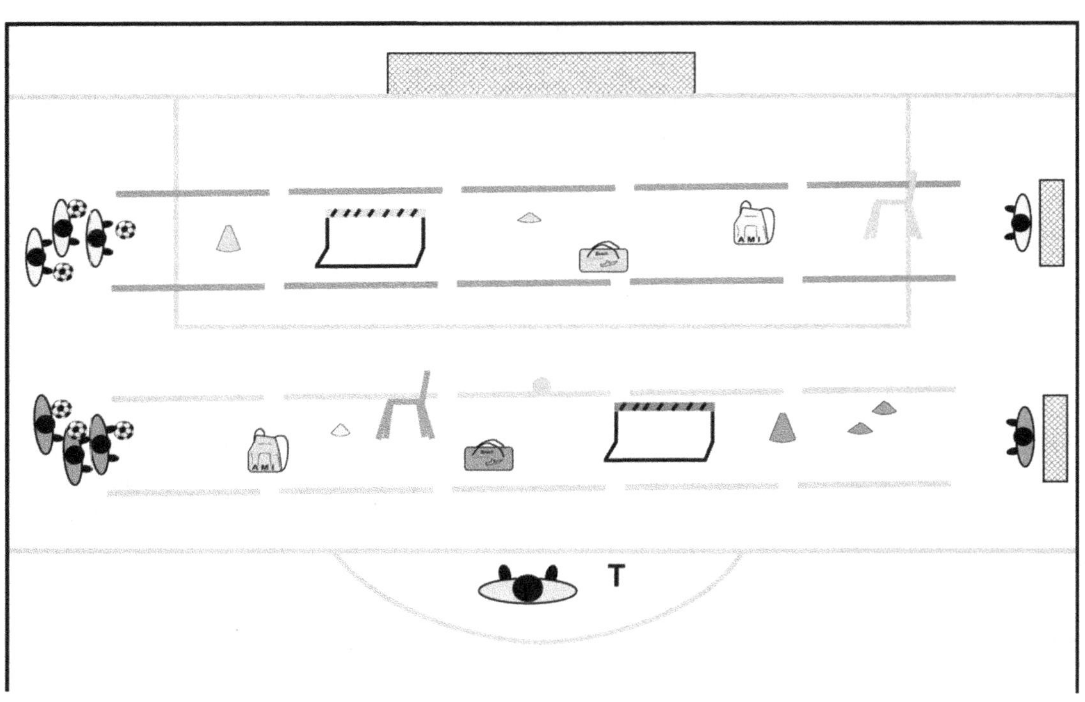

AMI
AMI
T

THE THREE CONES

OBJECTIVES

Increasing speed of performance.
Dribbling the ball with zigzagging movements.

EQUIPMENT

One ball per team.
Six cones and a few poles.

AREA OF PLAY

The penalty area.
Two squares are outlined inside the penalty area, each
near one of its shorter sides, by laying down a few poles.
Three cones are placed inside each square.
At a certain distance from the squares, three small goals
are formed by driving two poles into the ground for each
goal (see diagram).
In the space between the squares and the goals, a line of
poles is driven into the ground. The line of poles will be
used for a weaving ("slaloming") exercise. The distance
between each pole should be about 1-2 yards.

PLAYERS

The players are divided into two teams, team A and team
B, and on each team the players are numbered
sequentially.

ACTIVITY

The two teams are arranged in a row, each along one of
the two long sides of the penalty area. The players on
each team are lined up in numerical order. At the
beginning of the exercise, player 1 on each team places
himself in front of a square. When the coach gives the
signal, player 1 takes one cone from his square, and, after
dribbling the ball through the poles, places the cone
inside the first goal. Then he goes back to the square and
picks up another cone, bringing it to the second goal
while again dribbling and slaloming through the poles;
finally he picks up the third cone, and does the same,
placing it in the third goal. After placing the third cone in
the third goal, he passes the ball to player 2, who controls
it with the inside of the foot and performs the same
exercise, but in the reverse direction, dribbling and
slaloming through the line of poles. That is, he picks up
the cone from the third goal and carries it into the square,
and so on.
The game goes on like this until all the players have had
an opportunity.

If a player either throws the cone into the square or fails
to enter the goal in order to lay the cone on the ground,
he must repeat the leg. One point is scored by the team
whose players finish the exercise first.

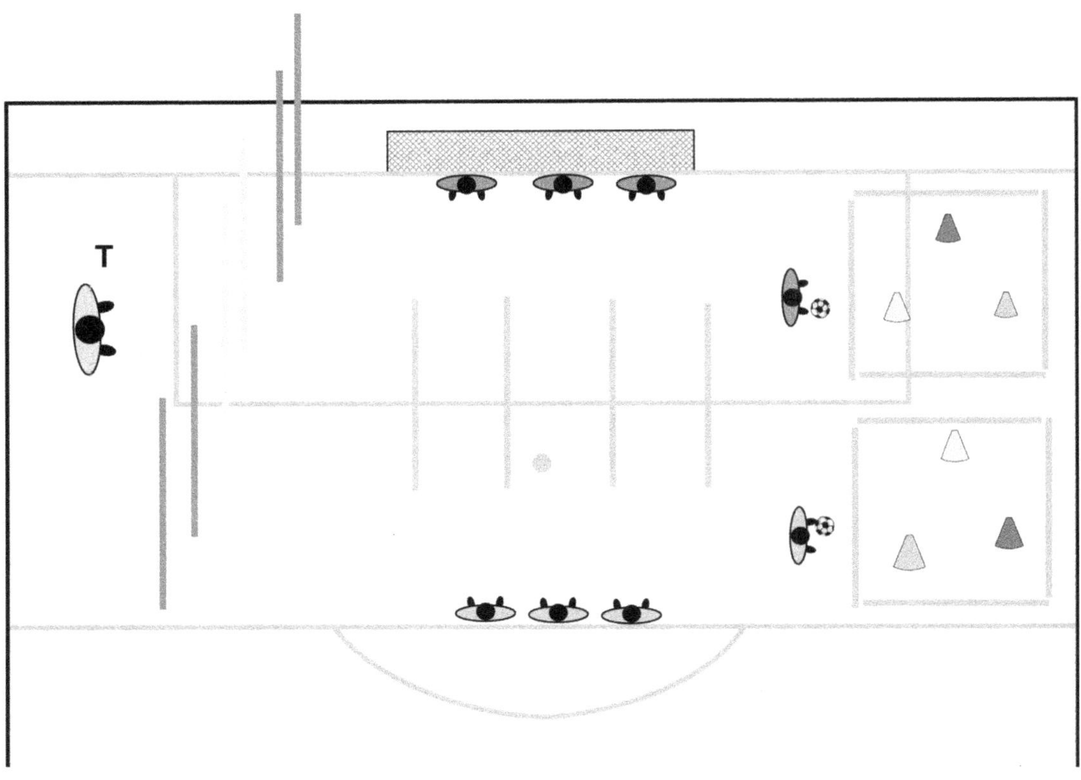

"STEAL THE BALL"

OBJECTIVES

Watching the ball.
Looking around.
Dribbling the ball.

EQUIPMENT

One ball for each player on one of the teams only.
A few cones.

AREA OF PLAY

The penalty area, or a space suitable for the number of players, but not too large. A number of cones equal to the number of players on one team is placed in the area of play, which is in the form of a triangle with three uneven sides and three uneven angles.

PLAYERS

The players are divided into two teams, team A and team B.

ACTIVITY

Each player on team A is sitting next to a cone, with his legs stretched forward. The objective of the A players is to steal the ball from their opponents, using either their legs or their arms. The B players each have a ball and are arranged in a row along one short side of the area of play. When the coach gives the signal, the B players dribble their balls to the opposite side of the area of play, while the A players, from their sitting positions, try to steal the balls using only their legs or arms.
One point is scored by the A players for each ball stolen.

ADVICE

The players should be asked to dribble the ball forward avoiding the spaces where there are too many opponents or teammates.

VARIATION

The players with the ball have a plastic tape hanging out from the back of their shorts like a tail. The plastic tape should touch the ground. When they cross the area of play, the opponents must try to steal their tail and not their ball. One point is scored by the A players for each stolen tail.

"SCORE AND GO BACK"

OBJECTIVES

Speed of performance.
Quickness of reflex.

EQUIPMENT

One ball for each player of one team.
A few cones.

AREA OF PLAY

A rectangular space.
A few cones, placed at about one third the distance from one of the long sides of the area of play, are used to form small goals.

PLAYERS

The players are divided into two teams, team A and team B, and on each team the players are numbered sequentially.

ACTIVITY

The teams are arranged in two rows, just outside the same short side of the area of play. The players of team A each have a ball and act as attackers; they are lined up a little closer to the short side of the area of play than are the team B players, and therefore they are also closer to the small goals than are the team B players. The team B players act as defenders. When the coach gives the signal, attacker 1 quickly starts dribbling the ball forward in an attempt to bring it into one of the small goals. Meanwhile, defender 1 starts running after him to prevent him from entering the goal. One point is scored by the attacker if he manages to take the ball into the goal. On the other hand, one point is scored by the defender if he manages to touch the ball before the attacker can take the ball into the goal. Finally, two points are scored by the attacker if, after entering the small goal, he also manages to dribble back to his starting position without the defender ever touching the ball. Then players 2 carry out the same exercise and so on. After all the players have completed the exercise, the teams exchange roles.

"PULL THE TAIL AWAY" - SIX

OBJECTIVES

Improving relationships; even while competing, there are no winners or losers.
Watching the ball and the coach.
Speed of performance.
Turning around.

EQUIPMENT

One ball for each player in group with the greater number of players.
Pieces of plastic tape.

AREA OF PLAY

The goal area, or a space suitable the number of players, but not too large.

PLAYERS

The players are divided into two groups, A and B; one of the two groups, for example A, is made up of only three players.

ACTIVITY

Group A is arranged just outside one of the short sides of the area of play; group B is arranged just outside the opposite side. The players of group B have a piece of plastic tape hanging out from the back of their shorts like a tail. The coach is facing the B players. When he gives the signal, he starts moving toward group A by walking backwards, to the left and to the right. Meanwhile, the B players dribble their balls following the orders given by the coach; when he raises his arms, they make an about turn to dribble back toward the starting point. To make the about turn, they turn to the right in the following way: they feint a pass with their right foot, and move the inside of their left foot toward the ball, as if to make a pass; instead, they touch the ball with the outside of the right foot, turn around (pivoting on the right foot) and dribble the ball to the starting point with their left foot. In this way, they get back to the starting point chased by the A players, who try to pull their "tails" away before they cross the line where they started. In the following repetitions, the players whose tails have been pulled away join group A. When all B players have lost their tails, the teams exchange roles.

"ATTACK - DEFEND"

OBJECTIVES

Tackling.
Feinting.

EQUIPMENT

One ball for each group of players.

AREA OF PLAY

A line of four rectangles is formed on the ground for each group. Each rectangle is about 2-3 x 6-7 yards, and the distance between the rectangles is about one yard. At each end of the line of rectangles two small goals are placed 2-3 yards from each other.

PLAYERS

The players are divided into groups of four players each; the players of each group are in turn divided into pairs, A-A1 and B-B1.

ACTIVITY

In each group of four, one pair acts as attackers and the other pair as defenders. Each of the four players in each group is placed in one of the four rectangles. They are arranged in such a way that they are alternated; that is, in the first rectangle there is an attacker (A), in the second rectangle there is a defender (B), in the third rectangle there is the other attacker of the pair (A1) and in the fourth rectangle there is the second defender of the pair (B1). When the coach gives the signal, A starts dribbling the ball from his rectangle and dribbles it into the next rectangle occupied by B. B tries to tackle him without leaving his rectangle; if A manages to dribble the ball past B, he passes it to A1 and goes back to his original rectangle. A1 then dribbles the ball into the fourth rectangle, the one defended by B1, and, if he manages to beat him, he kicks the ball into one of the small goals at the end, thus scoring a point. On the other hand, if the defender manages to steal the ball, he can shoot it into one of the two small goals on the opposite end, thus scoring a goal.
If it is B1 (the last defender) who shoots at goal, A can intercept the shot from his rectangle and restart his action.
Then the pairs exchange roles and positions.

ADVICE

The defender should be asked to keep his eyes on the ball and his upper body slightly bent forward, with his legs wide apart. The defender should try to force the opponent to dribble the ball toward the defender's favorite side.

<h1 style="text-align:center">"PASS AND SPRINT FORWARD"</h1>

OBJECTIVES

Teamwork.
One-two passes.

EQUIPMENT

One ball for each group of players.
Chalk powder and poles.

AREA OF PLAY

A square for each group is traced on the ground by using the chalk powder.
Each side of each square is divided in half by driving a pole into the ground at the mid-point of the side's line.

PLAYERS

The players are divided into groups of four players each.

ACTIVITY

In each group, one player (player A) is placed in the center of the square, while the other three players are placed on three of the four corners; one of them has the ball. The player with the ball dribbles it along the side of the square; when he reaches the pole he passes the ball with the inside of his foot to player A, and sprints forward to receive the return pass. When he receives the ball, he dribbles it and passes it to his teammate on the corner, taking his teammate's position. The teammate who receives the ball dribbles it in the same way, passing it to A, sprinting and receiving the return pass, and then dribbling the ball and passing it to his teammate on the next corner, taking his position, and so on. During the exercise, player A adapts his position in the center of the square to the position of the player with the ball, to make the pass easier. After a pre-established length of time, player A is replaced by a teammate.

WAYS TO DRIBBLE

A. The ball should be kept close to one's feet.
B. The players should alternate their feet when touching the ball, dribbling it to the left and to the right of the line of the square.

ADVICE

1. The groups should consist of players with a range of ability (from poor to excellent).
2. The coach should carefully check the teamwork of each group.
3. No player should dominate over the others.

When the player who is dribbling the ball receives the return pass from A, he passes it immediately on to his teammate on the corner instead of dribbling it toward him. The teammate on the corner moves forward to meet the ball, controls it with the inside of his foot and turns around. Then he dribbles the ball forward and, when he gets to the pole, passes to A and sprints forward to receive the return pass, then passes it immediately to the next teammate, and so on.

"PILE UP THE CONES"

OBJECTIVES

Speed of performance.
Dribbling the ball in a difficult situation.

EQUIPMENT

One ball for each team.
Several cones and various items of equipment.

AREA OF PLAY

The penalty area.
Piles, each containing an equal number of cones, are
arranged between the goal area and the penalty area.
Various items of equipment (or objects) and cones are
scattered in the goal area; the number of scattered cones
should be greater than all those arranged in piles
(see diagram).

PLAYERS

The players are divided into two teams, and the players
on each team are numbered sequentially.

ACTIVITY

Each team is lined up in numerical order just outside the
penalty area, in front of a pile of cones. When the coach
gives the signal, player 1 of each team starts with the ball
and picks a cone from the pile and holds it in his hand;
then, he dribbles the ball into the goal area, places the
cone on top of one of the cones scattered in the goal
area and picks up both cones. He then quickly dribbles
the ball back, holding in his hand the two stacked cones.
As he crosses the long side of the goal area, he passes the
ball to teammate 2 and goes to the back of the line where
he waits his next turn, still holding the stacked cones in
his hand. Player 2 dribbles the ball with the inside of his
foot, picks a cone from the pile, and does the same exercise as player 1, at the end of which he passes the ball to
teammate 3, and so on until the cones in the pile have
been taken. One point is scored by the team that is first
to complete the exercise by picking up and carrying off its
cones.

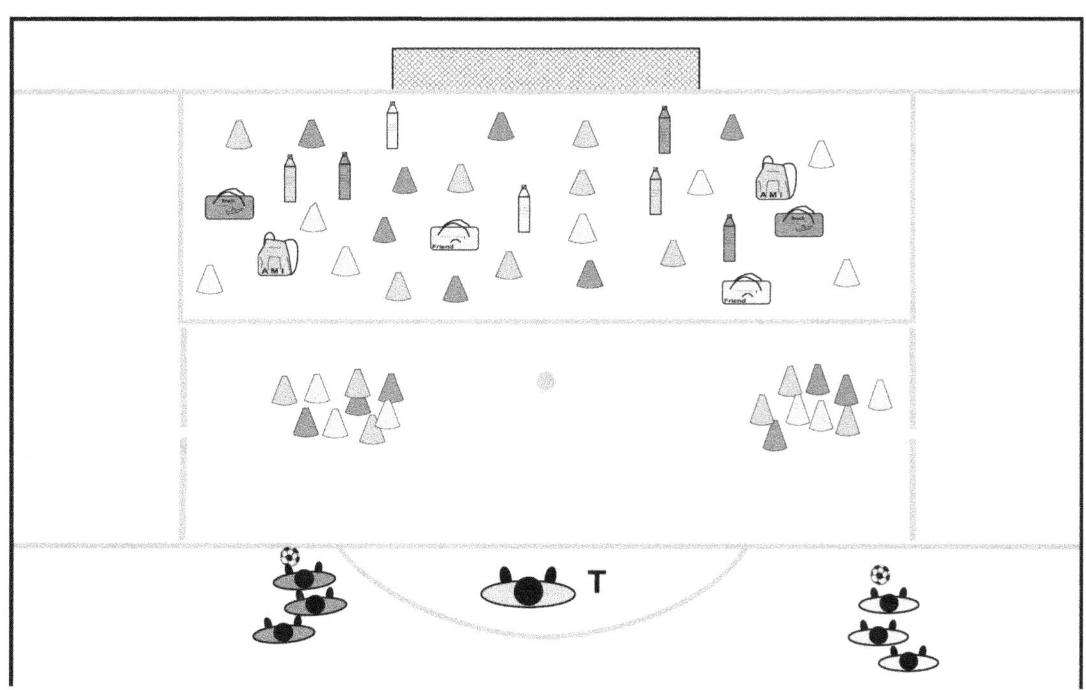

AMI
Friend
AMI
Friend
T

"RESPECT THE RULES"

OBJECTIVES	Development of motor schemes in relation to space and time:

OBJECTIVES

Development of motor schemes in relation to space and time:

- when dribbling the ball;
- when passing the ball;
- when trying to intercept a pass.

Respecting the rules.

EQUIPMENT

Cones, items of equipment, three balls.

AREA OF PLAY

A rectangular area the size of which should be suitable to the number of players.

Two large goals are placed in this rectangle, and behind each goal there is a circuit around which to dribble the ball.

PLAYERS

The players are divided into two teams.

ACTIVITY

Each team is arranged in its own assigned half of the rectangle. When the coach gives the signal, the players start playing a game in which they have to defend their goal and attack their opponents' goal. The player with the ball can keep it for only 7-8 seconds, and must then pass it to a teammate. A player who keeps the ball longer than 7-8 seconds is penalized by being sent off the field for a certain time. The players are allowed to steal the ball only by either intercepting a pass or getting possession if it goes out of bounds. If a player steals the ball by tackling the opponent, he is penalized and sent off the field to practice along the circuit behind the goal. A point is scored by a team when one of its players dribbles the ball across the opponents' goal line. The winner is the team with the highest score after the pre-established play time is over.

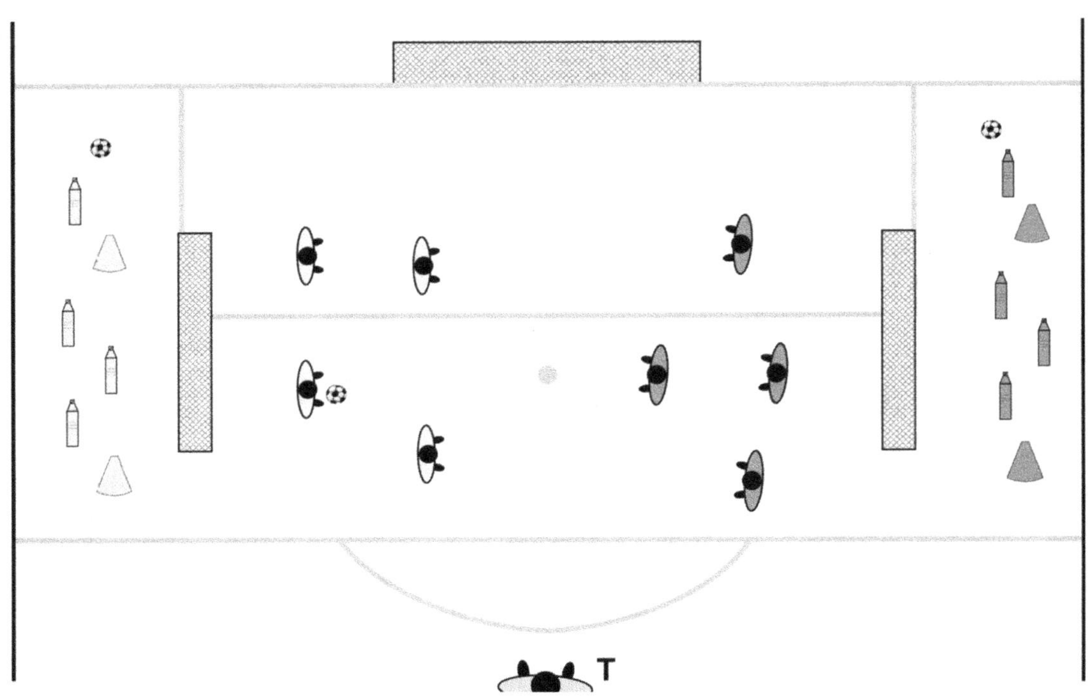

T

TRAPPING

OBJECTIVES

Improving relationships.
Improving coordination to accomplish a certain objective.
Improving teamwork.

EQUIPMENT

Cones and balls.

AREA OF PLAY

Three parallel lines of cones per group are arranged on the field; the distance between the lines is about 5-6 yards. In this way, two zones are formed: K and K1.

PLAYERS

The players are divided into groups of six or more players each.

ACTIVITY

Two players in each group, players A and A1, place themselves on the other side of the last line of cones, holding hands. The other players (players B) are opposite them, in front of the first line of cones (see diagram). Each B player has a ball. When A and A1 give the signal, the B players start dribbling their balls; they dribble them past zone K and, when they reach zone K1, dribble in the directions specified by A or A1. Suddenly, players A and A1, still holding hands, enter zone K1 to try to trap a B player with their arms; the B players try to avoid getting trapped and, if they are chased by A and A1, they can reach a safety area if, while dribbling their ball, they can get back to the starting point before getting trapped. Each B player who is trapped becomes an A player. The game continues until all B players have been trapped. Then the exercise begins again with two other players acting as A and A1.

ADVICE

Even though there is competition, this game involves real teamwork (the movements and the rules are simple; there are no losers, and there is competition without anybody acting as a group leader). Therefore, it is useful to make sure that the players are grouped in such a way that the group consists of players with a range of characteristics from the standpoint of speed.

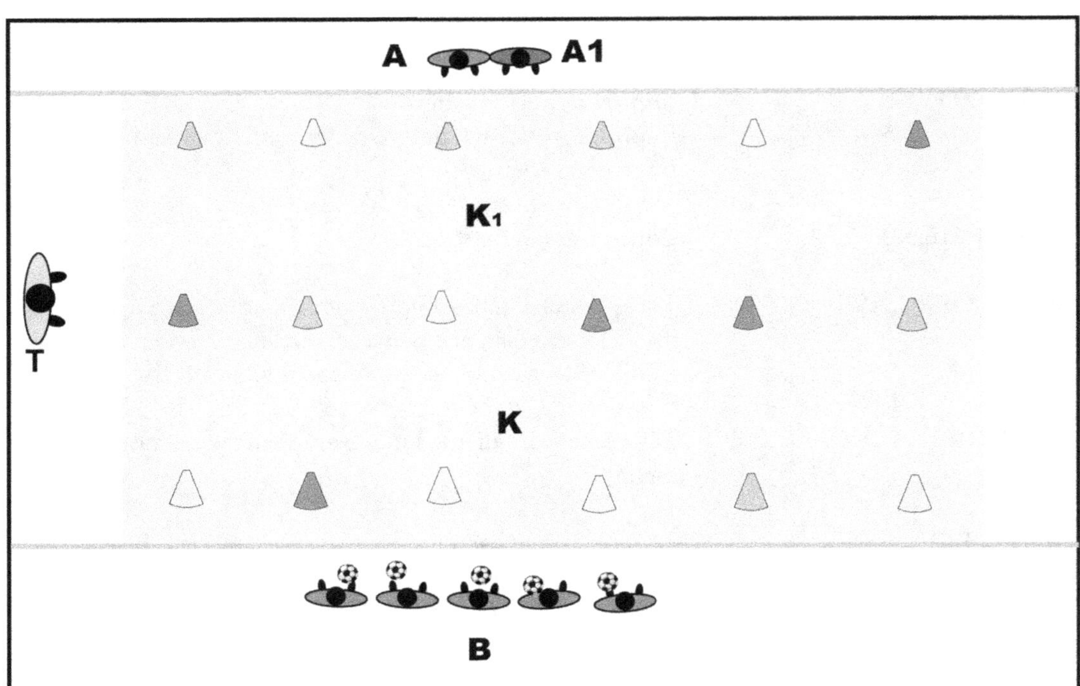
A
A1
K1
T
K
B

PICK UP AND COME BACK

OBJECTIVES

Speed of performance.
Control of the ball.
Awareness of surroundings.
Guided control.

EQUIPMENT

One ball per team.
Several pieces of plastic tape.
Two chairs.

AREA OF PLAY

The penalty area.
Several pieces of plastic tape are scattered inside in the penalty area, but not in the goal area. Two chairs are placed inside the goal area along the same line, at a distance of 10-15 yards from the longer side of the penalty area. The distance between the chairs is 5-6 yards.

PLAYERS

The players are divided into two teams and the players on each team are numbered sequentially.

ACTIVITY

The two teams are each lined up behind one of the two chairs. When the coach gives the signal, player 1 of each team quickly dribbles the ball toward the pieces of plastic tape; when he reaches one of them, he stops the ball with the inside of the right foot and picks up a piece of plastic tape, then dribbles the ball back with the left foot. As soon as player 1 crosses the long side of the goal area, he passes the ball to teammate 2, who moves sideways and forward to receive the ball with a guided control, then dribbles the ball forward to repeat the same exercise, at the end of which he passes the ball to teammate 3, and so on. The players stack the collected pieces of plastic tape on the chair. After putting the piece of plastic tape on the chair, the players go to the back of their line. The exercise finishes when the pieces of plastic tape have all been picked up.
The winner is the team that has collected the largest number of pieces of plastic tape.

"SEARCH AND YOU WILL FIND"

OBJECTIVES

Improving attention.
Improving memory.
Watching the opponent's action.
Speed of performance.

EQUIPMENT

Several cones (more than the number of players).
A number of pieces of plastic tape corresponding to the number of players.

AREA OF PLAY

The penalty area, in which several cones are scattered. Under some cones a piece of plastic tape has been placed. The players are not told under which cones.

PLAYERS

The players are divided into two teams, team A and team B. On each team, the players are numbered sequentially.

ACTIVITY

The two teams are arranged in a row, opposite each other, at the opposite ends of the area of play. Each time the coach calls out a number, the players in team A and in team B whose number corresponds to the called out number quickly dribble their ball toward the cones and, with the ball at their feet, raise the cones, one after the other, searching for the pieces of plastic tape. The player who is the first to find one scores a point for his team. The called out players have 20 seconds to find a piece of plastic tape, and the coach calls the seconds out loud. The game continues until all the pieces of plastic tape have been found.
Then, the coach hides the pieces of plastic tape under the cones again and the game restarts.

"LEAD YOUR TEAMMATE BY THE HAND"

OBJECTIVES

Adjusting to one's teammates' skills.
Speed of performance.

EQUIPMENT

One ball per player.

AREA OF PLAY

The goal area, in which several cones are scattered. The cones are meant to be obstacles to the player dribbling the ball.

PLAYERS

The players are divided into two teams. On each team, the players are numbered sequentially.

ACTIVITY

Players 1 of each team are arranged on one of the short sides of the goal area; opposite them, beyond the other short side, arranged in a line (which is not in numerical order, but random), are their respective teammates. When the coach gives the signal, each of the number 1 players quickly dribbles his ball toward his teammate 2. When he reaches his teammate 2, each number 1 player takes his teammate 2 by the hand, and, together, they dribble their two balls back until they cross the line from which player 1 started. There, player 1 stops and player 2 dribbles his ball back toward the line of his teammates and takes teammate 3, and then together they return to the other side, and 3 then will take teammate 4, and so on, until the entire team is now on the opposite side of the area of play.

One point is scored by the team that is the first to have all of its team on the side where player 1 started.

LIKE A STATUE

OBJECTIVES	Controlling one's body. Watching. Dribbling the ball: ● following a straight line; ● following a curved line; ● following a zigzagging line; ● following a broken line.
EQUIPMENT	One ball per player.
AREA OF PLAY	The goal area, or a space suitable to the number of players, but not too large.
PLAYERS	The players are scattered on the field, opposite the coach.
ACTIVITY	The coach chooses one player (player A) who the other players will have to imitate. All the players (except A) dribble the ball in the ways called out by the coach: following a straight line; following a curved line, drawing a kind of half-circle or drawing a wave-like path (a curved-straight-curved line); following a broken line (straight to the right, straight ahead, diagonally forward to the left, diagonally forward to the right, etc.); following a zigzagging line. Then, suddenly, the coach gives the pre-established visual signal (for example, raising his arms); player A chooses a position (for example, on his knees, on one foot, on his back, sitting with his hands on his head, etc.) and the other players must imitate him, keeping that position for ten seconds which are counted out loud by the coach. The players who do not immediately take that position or who do not keep it for 10 seconds are penalized: they have to practice for a pre-established length of time along a circuit previously arranged for this purpose outside the area of play. After a pre-established length of time, player A is replaced by another player.

"TOUCH YOUR TEAMMATE"

OBJECTIVES

Dribbling the ball in a difficult situation.
Individualized work.

EQUIPMENT

One ball per player.
Several cones.

AREA OF PLAY

The goal area or any other space suitable to the number of players, but not too large. Cones are scattered in this area of play.

PLAYERS

The players are scattered on the field.

ACTIVITY

One player (called player A) acts as a "chaser"; for a pre-established length of time, he must try to touch as many teammates as possible. Before the game starts, A places himself at a distance of 4-5 yards from his teammates. When the coach gives the signal, A dribbles his ball toward his teammates trying to touch them; they, in turn, dribble their balls around on the field, trying to avoid him. Whenever player A touches a player, the latter must pick up a cone and continue to dribble the ball while holding the cone in his hand, still trying to dribble away from A. When a player is touched for the fifth time, he must get off the field and practice at an individualized workstation. The workstations are individually assigned to the players before the beginning of the game. They should each be organized in such a way as to develop the same skill, but they should be different from each other in terms of difficulty; in other words, a workstation must be suitable to the level of skill of the player to whom it is assigned.

When the pre-established time for the repetition is over, the coach counts how many players are off the field (working at the workstations). Then, the "chaser" is replaced and the game starts again.

The number of repetitions should correspond to the number of players.

The winner is the player who has sent the highest number of players off the field.

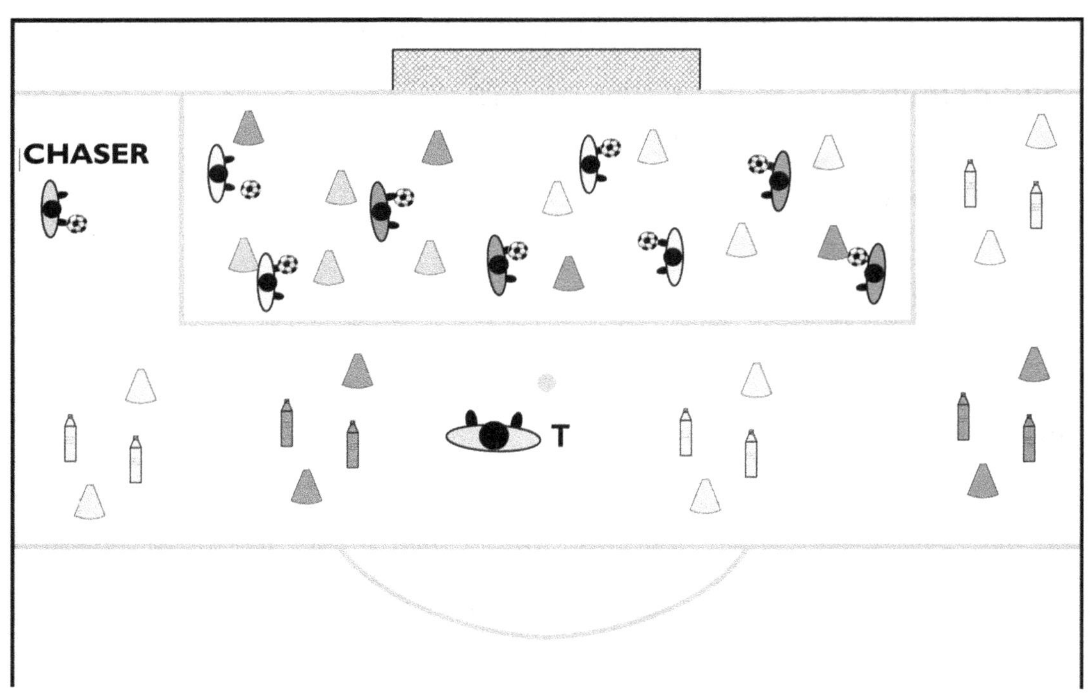

CHASER
T

TAIL HUNT

OBJECTIVES

Looking around.
Watching the ball.

EQUIPMENT

One ball per player.
Many pieces of plastic tape.

AREA OF PLAY

The goal area or any other space suitable to the number of players, but not too large.

PLAYERS

The players are scattered on the area of play.

ACTIVITY

At the beginning of the game, one player (player A) places himself at one end of the area of play (the players take turns acting as "player A"). The other players are at the opposite end and have pieces of plastic tape hanging out from the back of their shorts like tails. They "wear" their tails in such a way that player A cannot tell how many they have. In fact, the task of player A is to try to discern which player has a number of tails corresponding to the number called out by the coach. When the coach gives the signal, all the players start dribbling their balls in the area of play; meanwhile, the coach calls out a number, perhaps "3". Player A must dribble his ball among the other players, trying to spot which of them has three tails. When he finds him, he calls out his name and at that moment the repetition is over.

The number of repetitions should correspond to the number of players. The winner is the player who has required the shortest time to spot the player with the number of tails corresponding to the number called out by the coach.

"LOOK FOR THE TAPE"

OBJECTIVES

Individualized work.

EQUIPMENT

One ball per player.
One piece of plastic tape.

AREA OF PLAY

The goal area or any other space suitable to the number of players, but not too large.

PLAYERS

The players are scattered in the area of play.

ACTIVITY

One player (called player A) acts as a "chaser"; for a pre-established length of time, he must try to touch as many teammates as possible. He is placed at one end of the area of play, while the other players are placed at the opposite end, forming a circle around the coach, who holds in his closed fist a small piece of plastic tape. The coach passes, or pretends to pass, the piece of plastic tape from pocket to pocket of the B players and leaves it inside the pocket of one of them. When the coach gives the signal, the B players dribble their balls in the area of play, "chased" by player A who must touch the player that he thinks has the piece of plastic tape. When a player without the piece of plastic tape is touched, he leaves the game and practices at a workstation which has previously been arranged and assigned to that player before the beginning of the exercise. The workstations should each be organized in such a way as to develop the same skill, but they should be different from each other in terms of difficulty; in other words, a workstation must be suitable to the level of skill of the player to whom it is assigned. When the pre-established time for the repetition is over, the "chaser" is replaced and the game starts again.
The number of repetitions should correspond to the number of players, so that everybody can act as a "chaser".
The winner is the player who takes the shortest time to find out who has the piece of plastic tape

164

IN LINE - FOUR

OBJECTIVES

Individualized work.
Stimulating inventiveness.
Cooperating even while competing with each other.

EQUIPMENT

One ball per player.
Cones and poles.

AREA OF PLAY

The midfield circle, inside of which is arranged a number of circuits over which to dribble the ball; the number of circuits must be equal to the number of players. The circuits are formed with poles or cones arranged in such a way as to form letters of the alphabet.

PLAYERS

The players are each given a number.

ACTIVITY

Each player places himself near one of the circuits, except player A who is given number 1. The other numbers are assigned secretly to the other players. When the coach gives the signal, each player starts practicing at his circuit.
Meanwhile, player A dribbles his ball in the area of play and stops at the first circuit, then at the second, then at the third, etc. Every time he stops he asks the player who is practicing at that circuit what his number is, looking for the player whose number follows his own (in this case, number 2). When he finds number 2, number 2 leaves with him and together, while dribbling their two balls, they look for number 3. The game continues until a complete line of all the numbers, in numerical order, is formed, beginning with player A.
A number of repetitions corresponding to the number of players should be carried out, so that each player can act as "number 1". After each repetition, the players are given new numbers and exchange circuits.

ADVICE

The ball can be dribbled in different ways in the various circuits: from the left to the right, from the right to the left, or zigzagging through the cones.

TUNNEL - TWO

OBJECTIVES

Speed of performance.
Touching the ball purposefully.
Shooting at goal.

EQUIPMENT

One ball per player.

AREA OF PLAY

The penalty area.

PLAYERS

The players are divided into two teams, A and B, and are numbered sequentially. In addition, there must be a goal keeper who belongs to neither team.

ACTIVITY

The goalkeeper defends his goal. The players on team A take position in one half of the penalty area, and the players on team B in the other half. The players in each of the two teams are standing with their legs wide apart, with their balls in their hands or next to them. When the coach calls out a number, the players in the two teams whose numbers correspond to the called out number quickly dribble their balls to the opponents' half of the field, where they touch the ball purposefully to make it pass between the legs of one opponent after another. Each opponent sits down once the ball has passed under his legs, and once all the opponents are seated the player shoots at goal.

One point is scored by the player who shoots at goal first; if he scores he earns two points. The player who shoots at goal second scores a point only if he scores a goal.

After a pre-established number of repetitions, the winner is the team with the highest score.

"PULL THE TAIL AWAY" - SEVEN

OBJECTIVES

Watching the ball.
Watching the opponent.
Speed of performance.

EQUIPMENT

One ball per player.
A number of pieces of plastic tape corresponding to the number of players.

AREA OF PLAY

The penalty area, or a space suitable the number of players, but not too large.

PLAYERS

The players are divided into two teams.

ACTIVITY

All the players have a piece of plastic tape hanging out from the back of their shorts. Team B is arranged in a row along one of the short sides of the penalty area: Team A is arranged in a parallel way, facing team B, at a distance of 2-3 yards.
The coach designates a team A opponent for each B player and calls out his choices. When he gives the signal, each B player, while dribbling the ball, chases his designated opponent trying to pull away his tail.
Meanwhile, A players try to dribble away from B players. After 15-20 seconds the exercise is over and the roles are reversed: with A players chasing B players. One point is scored by the team that manages to pull away more tails from the opponents.

ADVICE

Players with comparable skill should be chosen as opponents.

IN LINE - FIVE

OBJECTIVES

Individualized work.
Stimulating inventiveness.

EQUIPMENT

One ball per player.
Cones and poles.

AREA OF PLAY

The penalty area, inside of which are a number of circuits for dribbling the ball. The number of circuits must be equal to the number of players. The circuits are formed with poles or cones arranged in such a way as to form letters of the alphabet.

PLAYERS

The players are numbered individually.

ACTIVITY

Each player places himself near one of the circuits, except player A who places himself near one post of the goal. The coach secretly assigns a number to each player. When the coach gives the signal, each player starts practicing at his circuit, while player A dribbles the ball inside the goal area. At a certain point he stops at the near post, where the coach has positioned himself; the coach calls out a number, and player A immediately starts dribbling the ball around the penalty area trying to identify the player whose number corresponds to the called out number. Circuit after circuit, he asks the player who is practicing at that circuit if his number is the one that has been called out. If it is not, that player continues practicing at his circuit, without telling him his number. On the other hand, if he does have the called out number, then that player lines up behind player A and leaves with him; together, while dribbling their balls, they go back to the coach who calls another number. Then, the two of them start dribbling their balls, looking for the player that corresponds to that number. Once they find him, that player lines up behind them and the three of them come back to the coach who calls out another number, and so on until a complete line, beginning with player A, has been formed.

The number of repetitions should correspond to the number of players, so that each player can act as "player A".

The winner is the player who takes the shortest time to complete the line behind him.

"CONQUER THE CONES"

OBJECTIVES	Watching the ball. Watching the opponent. Speed of performance. Getting the ball through the opponent's legs.
EQUIPMENT	One ball per player. Several cones.
AREA OF PLAY	The penalty area. On each of the two short sides of the penalty area, two poles are driven into the ground to form one goal (see diagram). An equal number of cones is placed in each of the two goals.
PLAYERS	The players are divided into two teams.
ACTIVITY	Team A is arranged on one half of the area of play in front of its assigned goal. Likewise, team B is arranged on the other half of the area of play in front of its designated goal. When the coach gives the signal, all the players must dribble their balls to the opposing half of the area of play, enter the opposing goal with the balls at their feet and pick up one cone. When a player has picked up a cone, he dribbles his ball back and puts the cone in his own goal. If a player is in the opposing half of the area of play without a cone in his hands and is touched by the opponents he must stop and stand still with his legs wide apart until one of his teammates frees him by dribbling his ball through his legs. One point is scored by the team that at the end of the exercise has the most cones in its own goal; one point is also scored by the team whose players have touched more opponents.

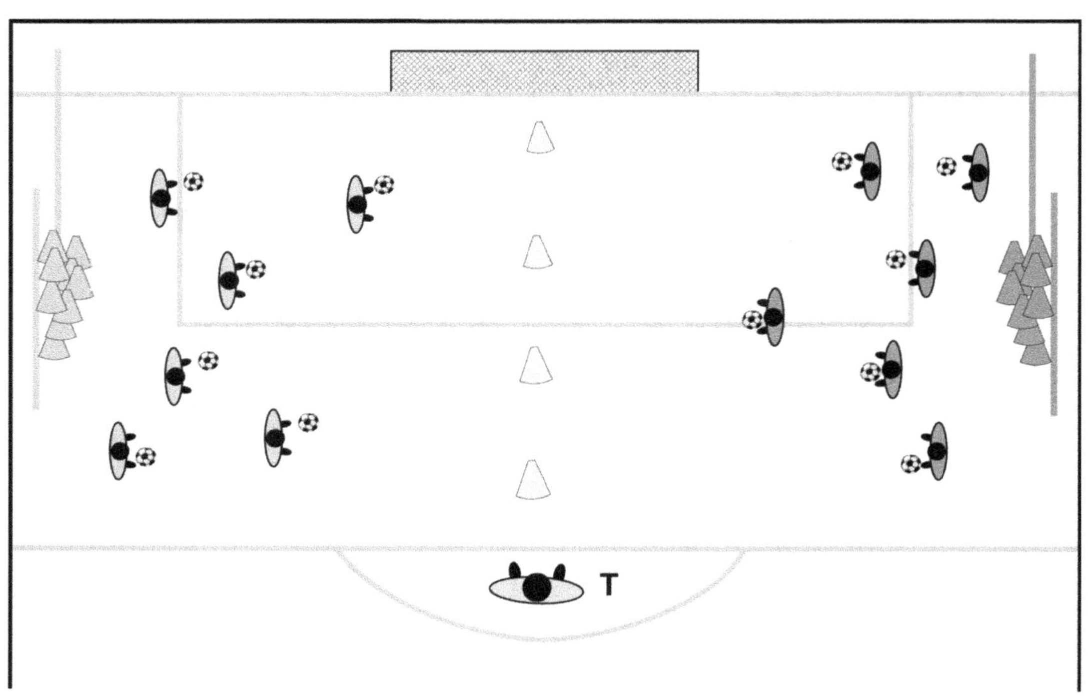

SET OF FIVE

OBJECTIVES

Dribbling the ball with zigzagging movements.
Speed of performance.
Controlling the ball and turning around.

EQUIPMENT

One ball per team.
Several cones or poles; clothes pins.
A bingo set.

AREA OF PLAY

A space suitable to the number of players.
Six cones per player are arranged in a line, 2 yards apart.
The lines are 6-7 yards apart and they form only one line per team.

PLAYERS

The players are divided into teams of three players each.

ACTIVITY

The coach has the bingo set in his hands and places himself among the teams. The first player on each team is standing at the first cone of the first line, with the ball at his feet. This is the starting and finishing point. He has 5 clothes pins clipped on his shirt. The second player of the team is placed next to the first cone of the second line. The third player of the team is placed next to the first cone of the third line. When the coach gives the signal, the first player of the team dribbles the team's ball by weaving through the cones making up his line; when he reaches the end of his line, he passes the ball to the second teammate and stops. The teammate who receives the ball controls it and turns around, and then dribbles it, weaving through the cones in his line. After the last cone, he passes the ball to the third teammate and stops. The third teammate dribbles the ball by weaving through the cones and when he gets to the end of his line he turns around and dribbles the ball back, weaving through the cones; when he reaches the last cone, he passes the ball to the second teammate, who dribbles the ball back by weaving through the cones and passes the ball to the first teammate. The first teammate dribbles the ball back by weaving through the cones of his line, until he reaches the last cone, which is where he started from, and puts a clothes pin on the ground. While the teams dribble the ball as described above, the coach pulls out some numbers from a bag and calls them out. When he calls a number which includes the number 9, the players who are dribbling the ball at that moment turn around and reverse their direction. When the coach calls out again a number containing the number 9, the players who are dribbling the ball at that moment turn around again and reverse their direction.

The player who puts the fifth clothes pin on the ground scores a point for his team by having a "set of five".

CATEGORIES

OBJECTIVES

Watching the ball.
Watching one's own teammate.
Controlling the ball.

EQUIPMENT

One ball per player.

AREA OF PLAY

The goal area.

PLAYERS

The players are divided into two groups that must play two different roles: the "watchful" ones and the "absent-minded" ones.

ACTIVITY

One player (player A) acts as an "observer". He places himself at one end of the area of play, while the other players are at the opposite end and are divided by the coach into two categories: the "watchful" and the "absent-minded". Player A does not know which player has been assigned to what category. The players in the two categories mix and place themselves in random order in front of the coach, who orders them to dribble their balls in prescribed directions. The players follow the orders according to the category to which they have been assigned: the "watchful" follow the orders immediately and exactly, while the "absent-minded" dribble their balls incorrectly, sometimes going in a direction opposite to the one ordered by the coach. Player A observes them while he is dribbling his ball in the directions ordered by the coach. Every now and then, the coach calls out the name of a player, and player A must guess to which category that player belongs.

After a pre-established length of time, player A is replaced and the players are divided again into categories. The winner is the "observer" who has the highest number of correct guesses.

MAPPING

(this exercise is suitable for the last training sessions, when the players know each other's characters, attitudes and tastes)

OBJECTIVES

Individual work.
Knowing one's own teammates and their relationship to the group.
Dribbling the ball while following a teammate.

EQUIPMENT

One ball per player.
Several cones.

AREA OF PLAY

The midfield circle.
A few cones are used to form a square in the center of the area of play.
Different circuits are arranged in the area of play at irregular intervals.

PLAYERS

The players are scattered on the field.

ACTIVITY

The players dribble their balls in the square in the center of the area of play. The coach chooses a player (player A), who chooses another player (player B). A places B near one of the circuits, following A's best notion of a "relationship map". That is, A uses the experience he has gained in the previous training sessions to assess the relationship among his coach, his teammates and himself. For example, if he thinks that B is a loner, he may decide that B may prefer the circuit that is farther away and more isolated from the others. Or, if he has learned that B is closer to some players than to others, he may place B next to them, and so on, trying to assess to which circuit would be best for B. Then A starts dribbling his ball around the circle and B dribbles his ball behind him until they reach the circuit to which A assigns him.
One after the other, A leads all his teammates to a circuit that he thinks is the most suitable for them. Then, A leads his teammates back to the square, one at a time, starting from B until the last one.
The players take turns acting as player A, and the game ends when all players have acted as player A.

CONTEST - TWO

OBJECTIVES

1 on 1.
Speed of performance.

EQUIPMENT

One ball per player on each team.
Pieces of plastic tape and poles.

AREA OF PLAY

The goal area.
A few poles are driven into the ground along the long side of goal area to form small goals. The distance between the poles is 3-4 yards. Behind each goal are some pieces of plastic tape.

PLAYERS

The players are divided into two teams: A and B.

ACTIVITY

Each player of team A is placed in one of the small goals to defend it. Team B, the attackers, are each arranged with a ball at their feet in front of an opponent. When the coach gives the signal, the B players try to dribble their balls past the defenders and, if successful, pick up a piece of plastic tape. Whenever a defender manages to steal the ball, he kicks it away into the goal area and the attacker must recover the ball and start again.

When the pre-established time is over, the coach counts the pieces of plastic tape that the attackers have picked up and the teams exchange roles.

The winner is the team to recover the most pieces of plastic tape.

THE CARRIER

OBJECTIVES

Control of the ball in a disadvantaged position.
Improving one's relationship with others.
Speed of performance.

EQUIPMENT

Two balls and a few cones.

AREA OF PLAY

The goal area, where two parallel lines of cones are
arranged. The distance between the lines is 4-5 yards.

PLAYERS

The players are divided into two teams.

ACTIVITY

Each team is assigned a line of cones. One of the short
sides of the goal area is the starting line. The teams are
both lined up behind this starting line, in front of the line
of cones assigned to that team. Two players, each with
the ball assigned to his team, are placed beyond the
opposite short side of the goal area. The line of that
short side represents the finishing line (see diagram).
When the coach gives the signal, the two players with the
ball start dribbling their balls, weaving through the cones,
and reach the line where their teammates have been
placed. They put one of their teammates on their back
and carry him to the finishing line, while dribbling the
ball through the cones. Once he has reached the finishing
line, the player who has been carried gets off the back of
his teammate and dribbles the ball back through the
cones toward the line where the other teammates are
waiting. He puts the next teammate on his back and
carries him to the finishing line. If the player who is
being carried touches the ground along the way, he goes
back to the starting point together with the player who is
carrying him and they start again.
One point is scored by the team that carries all its players
across the finish line first. The winner is the team that
gets to the pre-established score first.

ADVICE

The two teams and the two lines should be formed in
such a way as to prevent the smaller players from carrying
the bigger ones.

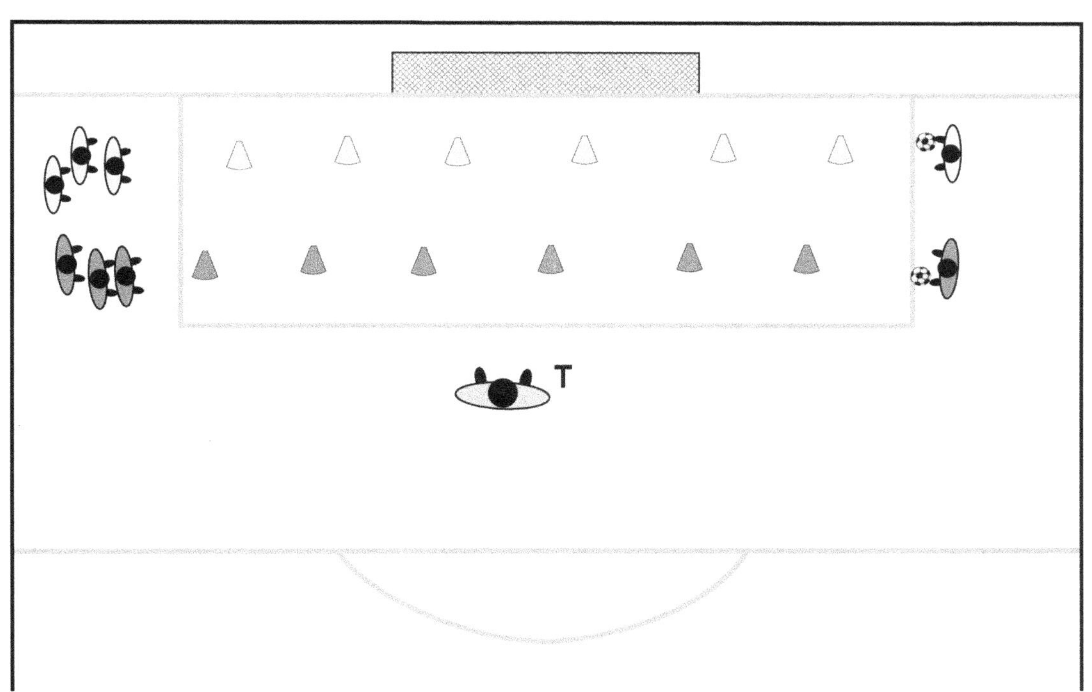

T

"BUILD UP THE CONES"

OBJECTIVES

Speed of performance.
Looking around.

EQUIPMENT

One ball per player.
Several small cones, small posts and regular sized cones.

AREA OF PLAY

The penalty area, which is divided into two parts by a stack of regular sized cones and small cones; in each of the two halves an equal number of small posts is driven into the ground here and there.

PLAYERS

The players are divided into two teams.

ACTIVITY

Each team is assigned one half of the area of play. When the coach gives the signal, each player dribbles his ball toward the stack of regular sized cones and small cones, picks up a regular sized cone and, while dribbling, places it next to one of the small posts driven into the ground. Then he dribbles the ball back to the stack of cones and small cones, picks up a small cone, and, while dribbling, places it on the cone which he previously put next to the small post. Only two cones - a regular sized cone and a small cone - may be placed at each post. The game continues with both teams piling up cones and small cones. One point is scored by the team that is the first to pile up a regular sized cone and a small cone next to each of the small posts on its portion of the area of play.

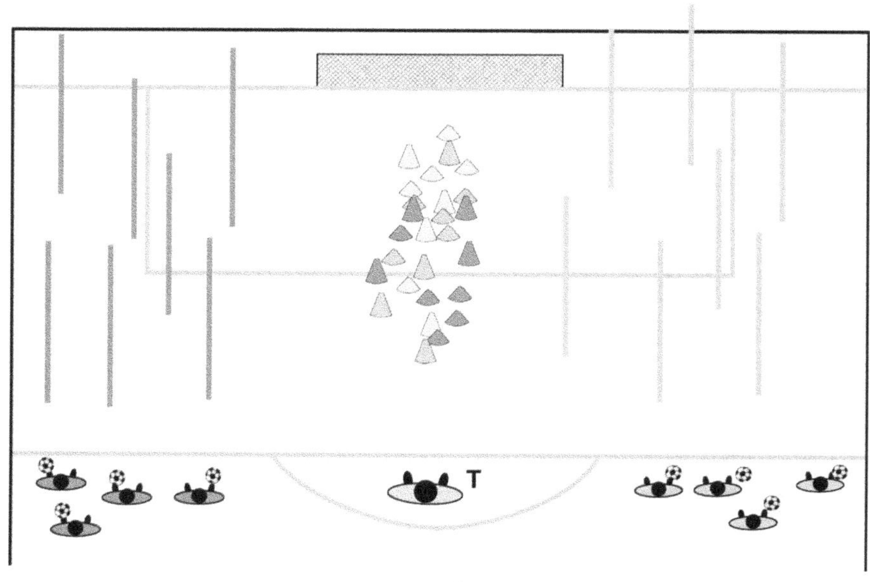

CONCLUSIONS

"Creative zigzags" is a collection of exercises and games which stem from games which some time ago were quite popular among kids, but which are slowly disappearing. The exercises have been adapted to develop motor skills and to improve both the dribbling of the ball, human skills, such as listening, establishing relationships, team working, and competing.

In my opinion, when a coach uses these exercises he should feel free to elaborate on them, and try to adapt them to the skills of his players. It is my belief that all the coaches will find inspiration and useful material in the simple ideas I have provided in this book. It is my hope that the application of these ideas in the exercises of soccer players will make their training activity creative, interesting and enjoyable.

Also Available from Reedswain

#149 **Soccer Tactics**
by Massimo Lucchesi
$12.95

#243 **Coaching Team Shape**
by Emilio Cecchini
$12.95

#249 **Coaching the 3-4-3**
by Massimo Lucchesi
$12.95

#256 **The Creative Dribbler**
by Peter Schreiner
$14.95

#265 **Coordination, Agility and Speed Training for Soccer**
by Peter Schreiner
$14.95

#816 **Playing Out of Your Mind**
by Dr. Alan Goldberg
$9.95

#905 **Soccer Strategies**
by Robyn Jones and Tom Tranter
$12.95

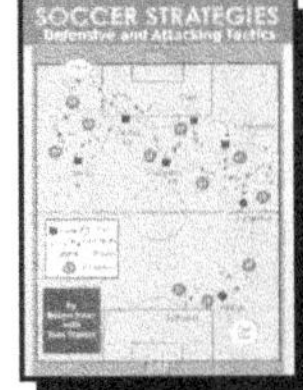

plus HUNDREDS more!

www.reedswain.com or 800-331-5191

9 781591 640639